A SELECTION OF TESTIMONIES ON HEAVEN AND HELL!

WHERE WILL YOU SPEND YOUR ETERNITY?

Where Will You Spend Your Eternity? : A Selection of Testimonies on Heaven and Hell!

Original Korean edition published in Korea by HolyPearl Publications.
First published in Korea under the title of 당신의 영원을 어디서 보낼 것인가?

Copyright © 2022 by Seung-woo Byun
Published by HolyPearl Publications
27-22, Wiryeseong-daero 22-gil Songpa-gu Seoul, Republic of Korea

All rights reserved. No part of this publication may be reproduced, stored in a retrieval system, or transmitted in any form by any means, electronic, mechanical, photocopy, recording, or otherwise, without the prior permission of the publisher.

All Scripture quotations, unless otherwise indicated, are taken from the ESV® Bible (The Holy Bible, English Standard Version®), copyright © 2001 by Crossway Bibles, a publishing ministry of Good News Publishers. Used by permission. All rights reserved.

Scripture quotations marked NASB are taken from the New American Standard Bible®, Copyright 1960, 1962, 1963, 1968, 1971, 1972, 1973, 1975, 1977, 1995 by The Lockman Foundation. Used by permission. (www.Lockman.org). All rights reserved.

Scripture marked KJV are taken from the King James Version.

Translated by HolyPearl Publications
Cover design by Jungmin Yoon

Website
www.belovedc.com
www.belovedc.com/en

Youtube
www.youtube.com/user/gfctvmedia

E-mail
holypearlpubl@gmail.com

ISBN 979-11-6890-030-1 03230
First printing, March 2023
Printed in Korea

A SELECTION OF TESTIMONIES ON HEAVEN AND HELL!

WHERE WILL YOU SPEND YOUR ETERNITY?

HOLYPEARL

CONTENTS

Forward — 4

1. Sadhu Sundar Singh — 10
   Life and Death — 11
   What Happens at Death? — 12
   The World of Spirits — 14
   The Judgment of Sinners — 17
   The State of the Rightous and Their Glorious End — 21
   The Aim and Purpose of Creation — 29

2. Marietta Davis — 35
   The Angel of Peace — 36
   At the Gate of Death — 39
   The Welcome of Heaven — 43
   A Boy Grown Up in Heaven — 46
   The Majestic Scenery of Heaven — 49
   Descending to Hell — 51
   The Desperation of the Lost — 53
   The Faithless — 56
   The Heavenly Melody — 63

3. Dr. Richard E. Eby — 70
   I Never Give Up — 70
   In My Father's House — 72
   The Sights of Paradise — 73
   My Peace I Give — 77

4. Jean Darnall's Mother — 85
   An Unusal Message Given to Mother — 86
   Mother's Sudden Death — 87
   Came Back to Life — 90
   The Heaven Mother Experienced! — 92
   A Solid Evidence Supporting Her Testimony! — 98

5. Elder-Deaconess Yeon-eui Nam — 101

The Faith of a Little Girl	101
The Guidance of God and the Test	103
The Persecution from Family and Marriage	104
The Devout Faith of Yeon-Eui Nam	109
The Death Sentence and the Glorious Death	112
The Shoking Testimony of Yeon-eui Nam, Who Was Brought Back to Life	115
The Spirit of Repentance Strikes the Whole Family	131

6. Pastor Bob Jones — 136
Heaven Experienced Through 5 Senses	137
Hell Experienced Through 5 Senses	141

7. Elder Young-moon Park — 148
My Wayward Living in the Darkness	148
Heaven	153
Hell	163
The Judgment Seat	170
Will You Believe?	173

8. Pastor Ivan Tuttle — 175
Going to Hell	176
More of Hell	185
Arriving in Heaven	189
Angels, Music, and More	194
Deeper Experiences in Heaven	197
Back to Earth	203
Final Words	204

9. George Lennox — 206
Death of a Criminal	206
Unexpected Resuscitation	207
The Testimony of George Lenox	208

The Final Appeal! — 216

Forward
By Pastor Seung-woo Byun

To evangelize is to love. It is the greatest way to love your parents, your children, and your neighbors. When I was a pastoral intern, I compiled a book called *Good Seed and Clear Waters* for evangelizing. Recently, I wrote two more books for evangelism.

First, I published the book, *An Afterlife Plan More Important Than One's Retirement Plan*. It is a book based on a powerful sermon series for saving souls that I preached.

Next, I published the book, *The Living God Is Still Working Today!* I obeyed the heart that the Holy Spirit gave me, and edited the Africa mission report and other amazing miracles that happened during the missions in Africa together to publish it.

Both books were made to evangelize with. Yet, while praying not long ago, I felt the heart that I needed to gather together reputable heaven and hell testimonies to publish for evangelism. Thus, I obeyed and compiled this book.

Beloved, this book is not only handy for evangelizing to those who do not believe, but also great for waking up believers.

Therefore, you should read this book first. Then, you should gift this book to as many people as you can or let them borrow it. I hope that you will all go to heaven. And by doing the above, I hope you will be able to bring at least one more soul (that is more precious than all things) to heaven too.

What happens when we die? This is the greatest mystery we all ponder. On this topic, the Bible says the following. **"And just as it is appointed for man to die once, and after that comes judgment"** (Heb. 9:27). When we die, we will all receive God's judgment.

Then, what happens to us after we are judged? Jesus clearly shows us the answer in the parable of the rich man and Lazarus.

"There was a rich man who was clothed in purple and fine linen and who feasted sumptuously every day. And at his gate was laid a poor man named Lazarus, covered with sores, who desired to be fed with what fell from the rich man's table. Moreover, even the dogs came and licked his sores. The poor man died and was carried by the angels to Abraham's side. The rich man also died and was buried, and in Hades, being in torment, he lifted up his eyes and saw Abraham far off and Lazarus at his side. And he called out, 'Father Abraham, have mercy on me, and send Lazarus to dip the end of his finger in water and cool my tongue, for I am in anguish in this flame.' But Abraham said, 'Child, remember that you in your lifetime received your good things, and Lazarus in like manner bad things; but now he is comforted here, and you are in anguish. And besides all this, between us and you a great chasm has been fixed, in order that those who would pass from here to you may not be able, and none may cross from there to us.' And he said, 'Then I beg you, father, to send him to my father's house—for I have five brothers—so that he may warn them, lest they also come into this place of torment.' But Abraham said, 'They have Moses and the Prophets; let them hear them.' And he said, 'No, father Abraham, but if someone goes to them from the dead, they will repent.' He said to him, 'If they do not hear Moses and the Prophets, neither will they be convinced if someone should rise from the dead.'" (Luke 16:19-31)

The Bible shows that heaven and hell truly exist. And the reality of heaven and hell is not only shown in the Bible, but proven through the experiences of many people.

Paul testified saying, "Boasting is necessary, though it is not beneficial; but I will go on to visions and revelations of the Lord. I know a man in Christ, who fourteen years ago... was caught up to the third heaven"(2 Cor. 12:1-2, NASB). Like Paul, some people while living on this earth, have been allowed to see heaven and hell. There are actually more than you might think who have visited heaven and hell. I want to introduce to you the most biblical and believable stories from them. I do so in desperate hopes that not only will you all believe in Jesus and be saved, but that you might also have an upright Christian life and go to heaven.

1

Sadhu Sundar Singh

Sadhu Sundar Singh wrote many books on his experiences and one of them is the book, *Visions of the Spiritual World*. He said the following in the preface of this book.

"At Kotgarh, fourteen years ago, while I was praying, my eyes were opened to the Heavenly Vision. So vividly did I see it all that I thought I must have died, and that my soul had passed into the glory of heaven; but throughout the intervening years these visions have continued to enrich my life. I cannot call them up at will, but, usually when I am praying or meditating, sometimes as often as eight or ten times in a month, my spiritual eyes are opened to see within the heavens, and, for an hour or two, I walk in the glory of the heavenly sphere with Christ Jesus, and hold converse with angels and spirits."[1]

I would like to introduce to you all some of the important sections of the visions that Sundar Singh had.

LIFE AND DEATH

There is only one source of life—an infinite and almighty life, whose creative power gave life to all living things. All creatures live in Him and in Him will they remain forever. … **This life may change but it can never be destroyed,** and though the change from one form of existence into another is called Death, this never means that death finally ends life, or even that it adds to life, or takes away from it. …

Never! **If a man is not destroyed at death then at once the question arises, where will man exist after death, and in what state?** I shall attempt to give a brief explanation from my own visional experiences though it is not possible for me to describe all the things which I have seen in visions of the spiritual world, because the language and illustrations of this world

---

[1] Sadhu Sundar Singh, *Visions of the Spiritual World,* (FV Editions, 2019) 3-4.

are inadequate to express these spiritual realities; and the very attempt to reduce to ordinary language the glory of the things seen is likely to result in misunderstanding. I have, therefore, had to eliminate the account of all those subtle spiritual occurrences, for which only a spiritual language is adequate, and to take up only a few simple and instructive incidents that will prove profitable to all.

WHAT HAPPENS AT DEATH?

One day when I was praying alone, I suddenly found myself surrounded by a great concourse of spirit beings, or I might say that as soon as my spiritual eyes were opened I found myself bowed in the presence of a considerable company of saints and angels. At first I was somewhat abashed, when I saw their bright and glorious state and compared with them my own inferior quality. But I was at once put at ease by their real sympathy and love-inspired friendliness. … As we conversed together I received from them answers to my questions relating to my difficulties about many problems that puzzled me. My first inquiry was about **what happens at the time of dying and about the state of the soul after death**. To this one of the saints answered!

"Death is like sleep. There is no pain in the passing over, except in the case of a few bodily diseases and mental conditions. As an exhausted man is overcome by deep sleep, so comes the sleep of death to man. Death comes so suddenly to many, that it is only with great difficulty that they realise that they have left the material world, and entered this world of spirits. Bewildered by the many new things that they see around them, they imagine that they are visiting some country or city of the physical world, which they have not seen before. It is only when they have been more fully instructed, and realise that their spiritual body is different from their former material body, that they allow that they have, in fact, been transferred from the material world to the realm of spirits."

Another of the saints standing by added in reply to my question, "Many whose lives have not been yielded to God, when about to die, seem to become unconscious; but what actually happens is that when they see the hideous and devilish faces of the evil spirits that have come about them, they become speechless and paralysed by fear. On the other hand the dying of a believer is frequently the very opposite of this. He is extremely happy for he sees angels and saintly spirits coming to welcome him. Then too, his loved ones, who have died before, are permitted to attend his deathbed, and to conduct his soul to

the spiritual world. ... After that a fourth saint said, **"To conduct the souls of men from the world is the work of angels. ... But in some cases He Himself comes to a deathbed to welcome His servant and in love dries his tears, and leads him into Paradise.** As a child born into the world finds everything provided for its wants, so does the soul, on entering the spiritual world find all its wants supplied."

THE WORLD OF SPIRITS

Sons of Light

When the souls of men arrive in the world of spirits the good at once separate from the evil. In the world all are mixed together, but it is not so in the spiritual world. I have many times seen that **when the spirits of the good—the Sons of Light enter into the world of spirits they first of all bathe in the impalpable air-like waters of a crystal clear ocean, and in this they find an intense and exhilarating refreshment. Within these miraculous waters they move about as if in open air, neither are they drowned beneath them, nor do the waters wet them, but, wonderfully cleansed and refreshed and fully purified, they enter into the world of glory and light, where they will ever remain in the presence of their dear Lord, and in the fel-**

lowship of innumerable saints and angels.

Sons of Darkness

How different from these are the souls of those whose lives have been evil. Ill at ease in the company of the Sons of Light, and tormented by the all-revealing light of Glory, they struggle to hide themselves in places where their impure and sin-stained natures will not be seen. From the lowest and darkest part of the world of spirits a black and evil-smelling smoke arises, and in their effort to hide themselves from the light, these Sons of Darkness push down, and cast themselves headlong into it, and from it their bitter wails of remorse and anguish are heard constantly to arise.

Death of a Child

A little child died of pneumonia, and a party of angels came to conduct his soul to the world of spirits. I wish that his mother could have seen that wonderful sight, then, instead of weeping, she would have sung with joy, for the angels take care of the little ones with a care and a love that no mother ever could show.

Unseen Help

Our relatives and dear ones, and at times the saints as well often come from the unseen world to help and protect us, but the angels always do. Yet they have never been allowed to make themselves visible to us, except at a few times of very special need. By ways unrecognised by us they influence us towards holy thoughts, and incline us towards God and towards good conduct.

Who Is the Greatest?

The greatness of any one does not depend upon his knowledge and position, nor by these alone can any one be great. A man is as great as he can be useful to others, and the usefulness of his life to others depends on his service to them. Hence, in so far as a man can serve others in love, just so far is he great.

As the Lord said, "But whosoever will be great among you let him be your servant"(Matt. 20:26).

The Manifestation of Christ

For His glory is so surpassing that even the angels look on Him with difficulty, and cover their faces with their wings (Isaiah 6:9). When He does reveal Himself to any one He takes into account the particular stage of progress to which that soul has attained, so He appears dimly, or in the fuller light of His glory, that the sight of Him may be endured.

A Labourer and a Doubter

Once I saw in a vision a labouring man arrive in the spirit world. He was in great distress, for in all his life he had given no thought to anything but earning his daily bread. He had been too busy to think of God, or of spiritual things. At the same time he had died another had also died, who was a doubter, obstinate in his opinions. Both were ordered to remain for a long period far down in the world of spirits in a place of darkness.

THE JUDGMENT OF SINNERS

Many have the idea that if they sin in secret then none will ever know about it, but it is altogether impossible that any sin should remain hidden forever. At some time or other it will certainly be known, and the sinner will also receive the punishment he deserves. Also goodness and truth can never be hidden. In the end they must triumph, though, for a time, they may not be recognised (1 Timothy 5:24-25).

Secret Sins

The following was also related to me in a vision. A man in the secret of his own room was committing a sinful act, and he thought that his sin was hidden. One of the saints said, "**How I wish that the spiritual eyes of this man had been open at the time, then he would never have dared to commit this sin." For in that room were a number of angels and saints, as well as some spirits of his dear ones, who had come to help him. All of them were grieved to see his shameful conducts and one of them said, "We came to help him, but now we will have to be witnesses against him at the time of his judgment. He cannot see us, but we can all see him indulging in this sin. Would that this man would repent, and be saved from the punishment to come."**

Wasted Opportunities

Once I saw in the world of spirits a spirit who, with cries of remorse was rushing about like a madman.

An angel said, "**In the world this man had many chances of repenting and turning towards God, but whenever his conscience began to trouble him he used to drown its prickings in drink. He wasted all his property, and ruined his family, and in the end committed suicide, and now in the world of spirits he rushes frantically about like a mad dog and writhes in remorse at the thought of his lost opportunities."**

The Spirit of a Murderer

A man, who some years before had killed a Christian preacher, was bitten by a snake in the jungle, and died. When he entered the world of spirits, he saw good and bad spirits all around him, and because the whole aspect of his soul showed that he was a son of darkness, the evil spirits soon had possession of him, and pushed him along with them towards the darkness.

The Spirit of a Liar

In the world there was a man so addicted to lying that it had become second nature to him. When he died and entered the world of spirits, he tried to lie as usual, but was greatly ashamed because even before he could speak, his thoughts were known to all. No one can be a hypocrite there, because the thought of no heart can remain hidden. The soul as it leaves the body bears in it the imprint of all its sin, and its very members become witnesses against it. Nothing can blot out that stain of sin except the blood of Christ. … I watched him as, inextricably tangled in his own deceit, he turned his face away from the light from above, and hurried away far down into the darkness.

The Spirit of an Adulterer

I saw an adulterer, who had shortly before arrived in the world of spirits. His tongue was hanging out like a man consumed by thirst, his nostrils were distended, and he beat his arms about as if a kind of fire burned within him. His appearance was so evil and loathsome that I revolted at looking at him. All the accompaniments of luxury and sensuality had been left behind in the world and now, like a mad dog, he ran frantically around, and cried, **"Curse on this life! There is no death here to put an end to all this pain. And here the spirit cannot die, otherwise, I should again kill myself, as I did with a pistol in the world in order to escape from my troubles there. But this pain is far greater than the pain of the world. What shall I do?"**

Saying this he ran towards the darkness, where were many other like minded spirits, and there disappeared. One of the saints said **"Not only is an evil act sin, but an evil thought, and an evil look is also sin. This sin is not confined only to trafficking with strange women, but excess and animalism in relation to one's wife is also sin (1 Thessalonians 4:4)."**

The Soul of a Robber

A robber died and entered the world of spirits. At first he took no interest in his state, or in the spirits about him, but, as his habit was, he at once set about helping himself to the valuables of the place. But he was amazed that in the spirit world the very things seemed to be speaking and accusing him of his unworthy action.

After this the angels appointed to the duty took him, and shut him down in the darkness from which he is not permitted to come out. The state of evildoers in that place is so terrible, and so inexpressibly fierce is this torment, that those who see them tremble at the sight. Because of the limitations of our worldly speech we can only say this, that **wherever the soul of a sinner is, always and in every way, there is nothing but pain that ceases not for a moment. A kind of lightless fire burns forever and torments these souls, but neither are they altogether consumed, nor does the fire die out** (Mark 9:43-49).

In the dark part of the world of spirits, **which is called Hell, there are many grades and planes, and the particular one in which any spirit lives in suffering is dependent on the quantity and character of his sins.**

THE STATE OF THE RIGHTEOUS AND THEIR GLORIOUS END

Heaven, or the Kingdom of God, begins in the lives of all

true believers in this world. Their hearts are always filled with peace and joy, no matter what persecutions and troubles they may have to endure; for God, who is the source of all peace and life, dwells in them. Death is no death for them, but a door by which they enter forever into their eternal home.

The Death of a Righteous Man

An angel related to me how a true Christian, who had wholeheartedly served his Master for thirty years, lay dying. A few minutes before he died God opened his spiritual eyes that, even before leaving the body, he might see the spiritual world and might tell what he saw to those about him. He saw that heaven had been opened for him, and a party of angels and saints was coming out to meet him, and at the door the Saviour with outstretched hand was waiting to receive him. As all this broke upon him he gave such a shout of joy that those at his bedside were startled.

"What a joy it is for me," he exclaimed, "I have long been waiting that I might see my Lord, and go to Him. Oh friends! look at His face all lighted by love, and see that company of angels that has come for me. What a glorious place it is! Friends, I am setting out for my real home, do not grieve over my departure, but rejoice!"

One of those present at his bedside said quietly, "His mind is wandering." He heard the low voice and said, "**No, it is not. I am quite conscious. I wish you could see this wonderful sight. I am sorry it is hidden from your eyes. Good-bye, we will meet again in the next world.**" Saying this he closed his eyes, and said, "Lord I commend my soul into thy hands." and so fell asleep.

Comforting His Dear Ones

As soon as his soul had left his body the angels took him in their arms, and were about to go off to heaven, but he asked them to delay a few minutes. He looked at his lifeless body, and at his friends, and said to the angels, "I did not know that the spirit after leaving the body could see his own body and his friends. I wish my friends could see me, as well as I can see them, then these would never count me as dead, nor mourn for me as they do."

Then he examined his spiritual body and found it beautifully light and delicate, and totally different from his gross material body. On that he began to restrain his wife and children who were weeping and kissing his cold body. He stretched out his delicate spiritual hands, and began to explain to them, and with great love to press them away from it, but they could neither see him, nor hear his voice…

Then one of the angels said, "Come, let us take you to your everlasting home. Do not be sorry for them. The Lord Himself, and we also, will comfort them. This separation is but for a few days." Then in company with the angels he set out for heaven. They had gone forward only a little way when another band of angels met them with cries of "Welcome." Many friends and dear ones, who had died before him, also met him, and on seeing them his joy was further increased. On reaching the gate of heaven the angels and saints stood in silence on either side. He entered, and in the doorway was met by Christ. At once he fell at His feet to worship Him, but the Lord lifted him up, and embraced him, and said, "Well done, good and faithful servant, enter thou into the joy of thy Lord (Matthew 25:21, 23)."

From his eyes tears of joy began to flow, and the Lord in great love wiped them away, and to the angels He said, **"Take him to that most glorious mansion that, from the beginning, has been prepared for him."**

Now the spirit of this man of God still held the earthly idea, that to turn his back on the Lord as he went off with the angels would be a dishonour to Him. He hesitated to do this, but, when at last he turned his face towards the mansion, he was astonished to see that wherever he looked he could see the Lord. For Christ is present in every place, and is seen everywhere by saints and angels. …**those who are lowest in rank meet without envy those who are higher, and that those whose position is more exalted count themselves fortunate to be able to serve their brethren in lower positions because this is the kingdom of God, and of love.** In every part of heaven there are superb gardens which all the time produce every variety of sweet and luscious fruit, and all kinds of sweet scented flowers that never fade. In them creatures of every kind give praise to God unceasingly. Birds, beautiful in hue, raise their sweet songs of praise, and such is the sweet singing of angels and saints that on hearing their songs a wonderful sense of rapture is experienced.

The Mansions of Heaven

Then I saw a man of God examining his appointed mansion from a great distance. When this man, in company with the angels, arrived at the door of his appointed mansion, he saw written on it in shining letters the word "Welcome," and from the letters themselves "Welcome, Welcome," in audible sound was repeated and repeated again. When he had entered his home, to his surprise he found the Lord there before him. At this his joy was more than we can describe, and he exclaimed, "I left the Lord's presence and came here at His command, but I find that the Lord Himself is here to dwell with me." **In the mansion was everything that his imagination could have conceived, and everyone was ready to serve him. In the near-by houses, saints, like-minded to himself, lived in happy fellowship. …this is the glorious future that awaits every true follower of Christ.**

A Proud Minister and a Humble Workman

A minister who looked on himself as an exceedingly learned and religious man died at a ripe old age. And without doubt he was a good man. When the angels came to take him to the place appointed for him by the Lord in the world of spirits. … **In that intermediate heaven there are grades upon grades right up to the higher heavens, and the grade into which any soul is admitted for instruction, is determined by the real goodness of his life on earth**. When the angels, who had put this minister in his grade, came back conducting in the other soul, for whom they had gone, they brought him up beyond the grade in which the minister was, on their way up to a higher plane. Seeing this the minister in a blustering voice called out, "What right have you to leave me half-way up to that glorious country, while You take this other man away up near to it? Neither in holiness, nor in anything else, am I in any way less than this man, or than you yourselves."

Then the instructing angels said, "... My friend, do not be offended if we speak plainly, for it is for your good. You think you are alone here, but the Lord is also here though you cannot see Him. The pride that you displayed when you said, 'I know all about it.' prevents you from seeing Him, and from going up higher. ..."

After this one of the angels told him, "The man who has just been promoted above you, was no learned or famous man. You did not look at him very carefully. He was a member of your own congregation. People hardly knew him at all, for he was an ordinary working man, and had little leisure from his work. But in his workshop many knew him as an industrious and honest worker. His Christian character was recognised by all who came in contact with him. In the war he was called up for service in France. There, one day, as he was helping a wounded comrade, he was struck by a bullet and killed. **Though his death was sudden he was ready for it, so he did not have to remain in the intermediate state as long as you will have to do. His promotion depends, not on favouritism, but on his spiritual worthiness. His life of prayer and humility, while he was in the world, prepared him to a great extent for the spiritual world.** Now he is rejoicing at having reached his appointed place, and is thanking and praising the Lord, who, in His mercy, has saved him, and given him eternal life."

Heavenly Life

In heaven no one can ever be a hypocrite, for all can see the lives of others as they are. ... There, their goodness is evident to all, and it ever increases more and more, for nothing is present that can hinder their growth, and everything that can sustain them is there to help them. **The degrees of goodness reached by the soul of a righteous man is known by the brightness that radiates from his whole appearance;** for character and nature show themselves in the form of various glowing rainbow-like colours of great glory. **In heaven there is no jealousy. All are glad to see the spiritual elevation and glory of others, and, without any motive of self seeking, try, at all times, truly to serve one another. All the innumerable gifts and blessings of heaven are for the common use of all. No one out of selfishness ever thinks of keeping anything for himself, and there is enough of everything for all.**

God, who is Love, is seen in the person of Jesus sitting on the throne in the highest heaven. From Him, who is the "Sun of Righteousness," and the "Light of the World," healing and life-giving rays and waves of light and love are seen flowing out through every saint and angel, and bringing to whatever they touch vitalising and vivifying power. There is in heaven neither east or west, nor north nor south, but for each individual soul or angel, Christ's throne appears as the centre of all things. There also are found every kind of sweet and delicious flower and fruit, and many kinds of spiritual food. While eating them an exquisite flavour and pleasure are experienced but, after the are assimilated, a delicate scent, which perfumes the air around, exudes from the pores of the body. **In short the will and desires of all the inhabitants of heaven are fulfilled in God**.

THE AIM AND PURPOSE OF CREATION

A few months ago I was lying alone in my room suffering acutely from an ulcer in my eye. The pain was so great that I could do no other work, so I spent the time in prayer and intercession. One day I had been thus engaged for only a few minutes, when the spiritual world was opened to me, and I found myself surrounded by numbers of angels. Immediately I forgot all my pain, for my whole attention was concentrated on them. I mention below a few other subjects on which we conversed together.

Names in Heaven

I asked them, "Can you tell me by what names you are known?"

One of the angels replied, **"Each of us has been given a new name, which none knows except the Lord and the one who has received it**(Rev. 2:17). **All of us here have served the Lord in different lands and in different ages, and there is no need that any know what our names are. Nor is there any necessity that we should tell our former earthly names. … And then we do not want people to know our names, lest they should imagine us great and give honour to us, instead of to the Lord**, who has so loved us that He has lifted us up out of our fallen state, and has brought us into our eternal home, where we will forever sing praises in His loving fellowship—and this is the object for which He has created us."

Seeing God

I asked again, "Do the angels and saints who live in the highest spheres of heaven, always look on the face of God? And, if they see Him, in what form and state does He appear?"

One of the saints said, "As the Lord Himself has said, "He that hath seen Me hath seen the Father"(John 14:9). **In this world of spirits the spiritual progress of any one governs the** degree to which he is able to know and feel God; and the Christ also reveals His glorious form to each one according to his spiritual enlightenment and capacity. If Christ were to appear in the same glorious light to the dwellers of the darkened lower spheres of the spiritual world, as he appears to those in the higher planes, then they would not be able to bear it. So He tempers the glory of His manifestation to the state of progress, and to the capacity, of each individual soul."

Distance in Heaven

I asked, "How far from one another are the various heavenly spheres of existence? If one cannot go to stay in other spheres is he permitted to visit them?"

Then one of the saints said, **"The place of residence is appointed for each soul in that plane to which his spiritual development has fitted him, but for short periods he can go to visit other spheres. When those of the higher spheres come down to the lower, a kind of spiritual covering is given to them, that the glory of their appearance may not be disconcerting to the inhabitants of the lower and darker spheres. So when one from a lower sphere goes to a higher, he also gets a kind of spiritual covering that he may be able to bear the light and glory of that place."** In heaven distance is never felt by any one, for as soon as one forms the wish to go to a certain place he at once finds himself there. Distances are felt only in the material world. If one wishes to see a saint in another sphere, either he himself is transported there in a moment of thought, or at once the distant saint arrives in his presence.

Is Man a Free Agent?

Again I asked, **"Would it not have been far better if God had created man and all creation perfect, for then man could neither have committed sin, nor because of sin would there have been so much sorrow and suffering in the world; but now, in a creation made subject to vanity, we have all kinds of suffering to undergo?"**

An angel who had come from the highest grades of heaven, and occupied a high position there, replied, "**God has not made man like a machine, which would work automatically; nor has He fixed his destiny as in the case of the stars and planets, that may not move out of their appointed course, but He has made man in His own image and likeness, a free agent, possessed of understanding, determination, and power to act independently, hence he is superior to all other created things. Had man not been created a free agent he would not have been able to enjoy God's presence… like the stars that swing un-**

knowingly through infinite space. But man, being a free agent, is by the constitution of his nature, opposed to this kind of soulless perfection—and a perfection of this kind would really have been imperfection—for such a man would have been a mere slave whose very perfection had compelled him to certain acts, in the doing of which he could have had no enjoyment, because he had no choice of his own. To him there would be no difference between a God and a stone."

The Manifestation of God's Love

Then another of the saints said, "**All the inhabitants of heaven know that God is Love, but it had been hidden from all eternity that His love is so wonderful that He would become man to save sinners, and for their cleansing would die on the Cross. He suffered thus that He might save men, and all creation, which is in subjection to vanity. Thus God, in becoming man, has shown His heart to His children, but had any other means been used His infinite love would have remained forever hidden.**

The angels also conversed with me about many other matters, but it is impossible to record them, because, not only is there in the world no language, no simile, by which I could express the meaning of those very deep spiritual truths, but also they did not wish me to attempt it, for no one without spiritual experience can understand them, so in that case, there is the fear that, instead of their being a help, they would be to many a cause of misunderstanding and error.[2]

---

[2] Sadhu Sundar Singh, *The Visions of Sadhu Sundar Singh of India*, (n.d.), https://livres-mystiques.com/partieTEXTES/SundarSing/visions.html

2

Marietta Davis

When Marietta Davis' story was published, people were considerably shocked. The public response was explosive. Due to this, her story instantly spread all over America. It has been over 100 years since then, yet Davis' book is still loved by many and continues to be published. I want to start at the preface of her book to introduce her story before going into the details.

"In the summer of 1848, a twenty-five-year-old woman named Marietta Davis fell into a deep sleep or trance for nine days. All endeavors on the part of her friends and physicians failed to arouse her from this unnatural state. When at last she awoke to a consciousness of external things, she was in full possession of all her natural faculties, with an almost supernatural acuteness of perception added beyond that.

Before she fell into the trance, she had been considerably troubled in regard to her future eternal state and was greatly disturbed by some lingering doubts. Her mother and sisters were exemplary members of a Baptist church in Berlin, New York, where they all resided, but Marietta's doubt seemed to have kept her from the enjoyment of the hope in which her family so confidently rested.

But when she came out of the trance, it was with joy and rejoicing over the unspeakable things that she had seen and heard., Her mouth was filled with praises to God, and her heart swelled with gratitude to Him for His loving-kindness. Marietta declared that while her body lay as if it were in death, her spirit had visited the eternal world."[3]

THE ANGEL OF PEACE

"What is happening to me?" The thought exploded in my mind as I reeled at the sight of the vast, bottomless deep beneath me. "Am I dreaming? Am I dead? Am I alive?" A thousand questions raced through my mind as strange unidenti-

---

[3] Marietta Davis, *Caught Up Into Heaven*, (New Kensington, PA: Whitaker House, 1999) 7.

fiable objects floated around me. I blinked, trying to clear my vision, but it was like a wild dream, with no familiar point of reference to which I could anchor my sanity. "Help me! Help me!" My cry erupted from my deepest being as I gazed in despair at the endless, trackless space around me and struggled in vain to return to the security of my country, my home, and my family.

A brilliant light appeared far above me. Like a giant star, its shaft of light thrust back the gloom as it steadily descended. My whole being was bathed in a glorious glow.

Gingerly I moved closer as it resolved itself into the most magnificent being I had ever seen. On her head was a crown of clustered jewels of light. In her left hand she held a simple cross. A saber of light was grasped in her right hand, and as she advanced toward me, light streamed from it and touched me. Instantly a whole new world of sensations filled my being. Fears and uncertainties were swept away, and I was filled with an overpowering desire to go with her. Yet, paralyzed with awe and wonder, I could only stand and stare. Oddly, all my mind could think of was, "What is her name?" But as I stood there gaping, she spoke.

"So, Marietta! You would like to know who I am?" She smiled. **"I am the Angel of Peace. I have been sent to show you**

what happens to humans when they leave this world. If you would like to know the answer to this question, follow me." …

My mind was racing. How did I get myself into this? What had I done to bring me to this alien place? …

For a long time before this I had wrestled with the great questions of life. A few things had become clearer as I had tossed them over and over in my mind, and I had reached a number of simple conclusions. These were: chasing money and fine things can never make you happy; relationships can let you down (no one is perfect); and many religious traditions are unreliable. … The more I had thought about these things, the more I realized that I could not find the answers by myself. I passionately wanted answers, especially to the biggest question of all: **"What happens to us when we die?"**

But I was unable to reach any satisfying conclusions. So it was, in the midst of this turmoil, that I found myself here on this strangest of strange days. …

"Follow me," said the angel, "but before you do, look back and see yourself."

I looked far below through the dark misty space and finally made out my motionless body. Gathered around me were my worried friends calling to me and frantically shaking me, trying every possible way to wake me, but without success.

"**This is the human view of life,**" said my angelic guide. "Look at your family. They love you and grieve for you. Every human goes through troubles and heartbreaks, and ultimately death. But the true picture of what happens after that is hidden from them.

"**Look out there at the world's teeming millions. They are full of hope, ambition, and troubles. Then finally, death arrives. All of them are afraid of death.** It is a ruthless destroyer and cuts life short. Generations come and go, one after another in rapid succession."

Timidly I asked a question. "**I know I am young and don't know much, but I have been thinking a lot about these things. One day all these people will die. What happens to them? Do they have a place to go to? Can you take me to them? Can I go and be with my loved ones who have already died?**"[4]

AT THE GATE OF DEATH

The angel spoke. "**Marietta, You have been given a special favor to learn about these things. First of all, let me tell you this. When people die, they are taken to the place where they will

---

[4] Dennis Prince & Nolene Prince. *Nine Days in Heaven: A True Story,* (Heatherton, VIC: RCM Publications, 2020) 5-8. Kindle Edition

spend the rest of eternity. However, the destiny of some is enormously different from the destiny of others."

As if to explain, she lifted her head and said, "Look up there. What can you see?"

I looked above me and saw a vast, shining heavenly place, brighter by far than the sun at its peak. Dazzling light radiated from it, shooting across the heavenly skies. I was spellbound and stared at it in wonder.

"There are many people up there you would love to see," said my guide. **"They wear soft white clothes and live in unalloyed happiness. There is no night, no sorrow or death, no sin or pain, no suffering of any kind."**

She was silent for a moment. **"However, before you see this, I have to show you some things that are not as pleasant.**

"Marietta, you are well aware that people on earth have widely different values and morals. You may not be aware that when they die and their spirit lives on, their moral nature is not changed. The bad are still bad, but the good continue to be good."

She touched my forehead, saying, "Tell me what you can see now." A new scene opened up before me—vivid and graphic. I saw endless crowds of all kinds of people struggling in the throes of death. Some were in majestic palaces, lying on beds spread with fine and costly coverings. Some were in poor, humble cottages, while others lay in dark prisons. Some were in lonely forests, others in barren deserts or on raging seas. Some lay under the scorching sun; others were perishing on bleak snow-covered mountains. Some were surrounded by weeping friends; others were dying alone and forgotten. Some had been murdered; others were killed on the battlefield.

This was **the place where time met eternity**, and it was a place of indescribable misery.

"**This is death,**" said my guide. "**It is the result of a divine law that has been broken.** But what you see here is only a small fraction of it."

She touched me with her saber of light, and as she did, I found I could see the immortal nature of all the dying people. I was able to see their spirits. I stood fascinated as I watched them leave their bodies and enter the regions of eternity, tentatively stepping out into new and untried experiences. ... **People of all classes and types were met—some by evil and wretched spirits, others by bright and holy angels sent from God.** This gateway of death was the common transition state between earth and eternity.

As the people left their bodies, they were attracted to spirits of a similar moral nature. Evil and unholy people joined

like-minded spirits and then moved off toward regions that were covered by dark clouds. People who loved good and had formed relationships with good people were escorted by holy angels to the heavenly glories above. ...

Once again she touched my eyes, and immediately above me, around me, and far away I saw spirits of pure light passing us, traveling at the speed of thought. "**These are serving angels**," my guide told me as they passed. "More than anything else they love to go on trips of mercy. They are protectors and messengers to people below them." ...

As the angel passed us, we moved silently in the same direction. I lost sight of the scenes below, and my attention was drawn by the bright light of the heaven that we were approaching.

We stopped on a plain filled with trees laden with fruit. We passed beneath their shady branches, and I heard birds singing. Their beautiful melodies filled me with delight. They were the sweetest songs I had ever heard. I thought we must have been on some planet, so I asked the angel its name.

"**This is the outer region of the spiritual paradise,**" she told me. "**These trees, flowers, and birds are so pure and refined that humans cannot see them. Their eyes are veiled from it all. Their hearing is dulled too, so they cannot hear the sounds. In** fact, they don't even believe such pure and perfect things exist. You can see and hear them because you have left your body and can now experience them through your spiritual senses.

"Remember," she said, "that this region is only the outer boundary of the home of spirits. These are the lower levels of the homes of those who have been made holy. When redeemed people die, this is the first place they are brought to. Here their guardian protectors teach them the basics of eternal life. They learn about heaven and pure love, which is love not contaminated by sin. They meet old friends here—those who have preceded them and have advanced spiritually to take on higher tasks. Family members can meet them here and talk with them for the first time. "This is the place where they first learn to sing the song of redeeming grace. They can rest here too and enjoy the pure atmosphere."[5]

THE WELCOME OF HEAVEN

We moved on until, in the distance, I say a domed pavilion of light. "That is the gate to the City of Peace," my guide told me. "We are going there now and … " She paused. "**You will meet**

---

[5] Prince & Prince. *Nine Days in Heaven*, 5-8. Kindle Edition

your Redeemer." She continued.

"It is a beautiful place. Angels live there, and also the people whom God has made holy. They love to play golden harps, lyres, and other stringed instruments. They sing the song of redemption over and over. It is the song of peace and never-ending love." ...

The gate was made of jasper and diamonds. It opened, and two angelic beings approached me. I was trembling with fear, but they each took me by the hand and led me toward another gate, which led directly to the pavilion of light. I could not speak. The sight of this perfect beauty and holiness was beyond description.

As I tried to take it all in, I was suddenly overcome by my sinful state and rebellious nature. My mind flooded with memories of past sins and doubts. Unable to cope with the sheer glory of everything around me, I fell to the ground. Then the angelic attendants gently picked me up and carried me through the elaborate doorway. **They placed me at the feet of the most glorious Being I could ever imagine. A crown of pure light rested on His head, and hair, white as snow, fell upon His shoulders. No words could begin to describe His splendor.**

An attending angel spoke quietly to me. "Marietta, this is your Redeemer. He is God. Yet He put aside His divinity and

came to earth as a man and suffered for your sins. He died for you outside the gate of Jerusalem. He died alone, just as it was written centuries before: '[he trod] the winepress alone.'"

I was totally overawed by Him. His goodness, tenderness, and love overwhelmed me. I bowed down, feeling that if I could only be considered worthy, I would worship Him.

He reached out His hand and lifted me up. **"Welcome, My child."**

The sound of His voice penetrated deep inside me and filled me with a joy that I cannot begin to describe. "Come for a while into the home of the redeemed," He said. ...

The moment was broken when a spirit moved out from the gathering and called my name, "Marietta!" I was overwhelmed to find myself in the embrace of someone I had loved very dearly on earth.

"Welcome," she cried. "Welcome to our home of peace." "Welcome, three times welcome!" echoed the music of a thousand voices. Others had gathered all around me, people I had known and loved on earth, all eager to greet me and hug me.

We found ourselves in a large beautiful room where we relaxed together as only old and familiar friends can do. I recognized all of them instantly, but they were very different from the way I remembered them on earth. I cannot describe them properly except to say that they seemed to be all mind, all light, all glory, all adoration, all love supremely pure, all peace, and calm serenity. All of these qualities were woven together in an awe-inspiring heavenly way.

They talked freely with each other, but not in human language. They spoke without sound, thought to thought and spirit to spirit. Ideas flowed from being to being, and **I learned there and then that in heaven you cannot hide things!**[6]

A BOY GROWN UP IN HEAVEN

As this scene passed from my view, the spirit who had kissed the cross motioned with her hand, and two children came forward. They each took her hand and smiled shyly at her. Turning to me, she said, **"These children died as babies. Being innocent ones, they were brought to paradise."**

The older one looked at me. **"Marietta, we are really happy to be able to talk to you because you will eventually go back to those who loved us and mourned when we died. When you see them again, would you please give a message to the man who is now sitting beside your body on earth? Tell him that although**

---

6 Ibid., 19-21.

our parents may grieve for us, we are free and extremely happy. Tell them that this is the only world we know. It was here that we first awoke to the reality of our existence. Our guardian angels take us to visit earth, but it is not at all like heaven. We see sorrow, pain, and death there. Here in heaven there is harmony, happiness, and life."

The boy became silent and looked down as if he was thinking deeply. I thought he seemed sad, but then I realized he was watching an angel coming up past us, close by. As I looked, I was overwhelmed by what I saw. Light covered her like beautifully made clothing, and she moved with perfect grace. I longed to follow her.

"Who is she?" I said. "She is so glorious—I can feel it. I would so much like to meet her." The spirit answered, "This is an angel who belongs to the infants' paradise. Do you remember reading in the Gospels what the Redeemer said concerning little children? It says, 'Their angels in heaven always see the face of my Father in heaven.'"(Matt. 18:10) …

Then I saw a completely different scene. Below me in a little room I saw a woman kneeling by the lifeless body of her dead child. Her body shook as she wept. Tears were streaming from her eyes. Then she stopped crying, and her face became like marble, her eyes set and glassy. Her whole body quivered as she pressed kiss after kiss on the cold cheek of her lost baby.

A man dressed in black entered solemnly and silently approached the weeping mother. Taking her hand he said, "Come, dear one. Try to understand that 'the LORD gave and the LORD has taken away; may the name of the LORD be praised.' (Job 1:21)

Remember that Jesus said, 'Let the little children come to me, and do not hinder them, for the kingdom of heaven belongs to such as these.' (Matt. 18:10) Jesus also told us that 'their angels in heaven always see the face of my Father in heaven.'" (Matt. 18:10)

The scene changed, and I saw the mother sitting beside a coffin with a gathering of people. She was staring at the ceiling, her face filled with grief. In front of the coffin stood the solemn man whom I had seen before. He read a psalm, prayed for the distressed, and then endeavored to encourage the mourners by explaining from the Bible that the baby, though dead, would live again and that an angel had taken it to Abraham's tender care.

The scene eventually faded, and the boy said to me, **"That lifeless form you just saw in the vision was my body, and the weeping woman was my mother. This is what happened after I left my body. The solemn man was a Christian minister. The** passing angel who paused before us just now was the one who carried me to the place prepared for young and fragile children. These angel spirits are continually nourishing their little minds."

THE MAJESTIC SCENERY OF HEAVEN

A voice above us called, **"Come up here!"**

A chariot-like cloud of light picked us up, and we rose inside a circular area rather like the interior of a tower. ...

A profound sense of peace and delight filled me as we emerged at the top. From here I could see the complete layout of the great city, stretching out on every side. Its beauty was breathtaking.

Built of the most precious materials, it was an architectural wonder, rising from the center of a vast circular lawn of soft, lush, green grass. Spaced at regular intervals were groups of majestic trees with luxuriant clusters of fragrant flowers. Beneath them in the open spaces were tiny garden beds filled with every variety of flower, blossoming shrubs, and vines.

Fountains of dancing waters caught my eye. Some bubbled up from the green grass to flow with a low and pleasant murmur through marble channels or beds of golden sand. Others gushed up very high, cascading down in streams that fed into basins. Some of these basins looked like diamonds, others like polished silver or the whitest pearl.

The circular lawn was surrounded by high, open trelliswork with a gateway at its eastern side. Flowing out through the gateway was a river, supplied by the fountains within. Looking around at the surrounding city, I noticed it was divided into twelve great divisions by this river. The river flowed in a spiral course, in twelve huge curves proceeding out from the center to the circumference. On each side of the river was a wide avenue, and twelve other straight streets intersected this spiral avenue. The straight streets began in the consecrated ground about the temple and radiated out to twelve equally divided points on the outer boundary. So the city was divided into 144 great suburbs, or divisions, arranged in increasing degrees of magnificence and beauty.

As my gaze followed the pathway of the flowing river and the stately avenues, I lost all sense of time and self-awareness. I had never seen anything like it in its splendor and complexity, and I became completely absorbed in studying it.

Each building in the city was extremely large and perfectly integrated with all the others. The entire city gave the impression of being one garden of flowers, one grove of shady trees, one gallery of sculptures, and one sea of fountains. All of these, together with the buildings, formed an unbroken expanse of sumptuous architecture set in a surrounding landscape of matching beauty. This was then overarched by a colored sky that bathed every object in its incredible and ever-changing shades.[7]

DESCENDING TO HELL

She touched my forehead, and immediately the brightness and glory vanished, and I began to descend. I found myself passing through a low and gloomy subterranean vault, surrounded by thick folds of darkness. A feeling of supernatural dread came over me, and I began to shake spasmodically. A terrible conflict rose up within me and filled my being. I was startled and confused, and my thoughts shattered into utter chaos.

As I fell further, I heard a distant roar. It sounded as if an ocean was pouring down some rocky cataract. I flailed about, trying in vain to grab something to slow my fall, which was taking me toward the awful abyss below.

At this moment a blue sulfurous flash lit up the darkness.

---

[7] Ibid., 31-40.

As it disappeared, I stared in disbelief as grim specters floated around me, enveloped by fires of evil. Gone were the holiness and peace that had surrounded the dwellers in paradise. The change was so sudden and dreadful that I could not think clearly. **My mind was flooded with horror and despair. I was terror-struck!** I turned to my guide for help, but she was gone!

Alone and in that dreadful place there are no means by which I can give even a faint idea of the agony of that moment. At first I thought I would pray, but as I began, my whole life flashed before me in an instant, and I realized I was utterly unworthy of God's favor.

I cried out, **"Oh! If I could have only one hour back on earth —for a time, just a brief time—to make myself fit for heaven!"**

Like a monster my conscience struck back at me. **"You had your chance! In your time on earth you turned your back on the provision God made for your sins. You completely rejected it!** Do you think now in this place of darkness and woe that your plea could possibly succeed?"

To add to my misery, all my previous doubts and skepticism then rose up like animals, glaring at me and encircling me in condemning mockery. All of my life's thoughts reared up with them. Not one of my secrets was hidden—they were all there.

THE DESPERATION OF THE LOST

With this, a gloomy black veil of night rose up from below. ... My doubts formed a cloud that shut out the glory from above and plunged me into a vortex of gloom. I fell rapidly, and the surrounding darkness opened to receive me. ...

I moved forward slowly and warily, as if I were treading on scorpions in the middle of red-hot coals. **The trees that waved about me were fiery blasts, and their blossoms were the sparkle of relentless flames. Each object caused me agony as I approached it.**

The phosphorescent glare surrounding each object burned my eyes. The fruit scorched my hand as I picked it and seared my lips as I tried to eat. The gathered flowers gave off a burning gas with a stinking, noxious odor that caused excruciating pain in my nostrils. ...the air that moved them was laden with disappointment and misery.

I turned to see if I could find even a single drop of water to quench my thirst. As I did, fountains appeared, and small streams flowed amongst the bushes and lay in calm and peaceful pools. However, I soon found that the pools were just another deception, and the spray from the "sparkling" fountains fell like drops of molten lead, making me recoil in horror. The

small flowing streams were like liquid metal from a furnace, and the deep, still pools were fiery silver in a glowing crucible, where every atom burns with an intolerable glow.

As I gazed aghast at these awful things, a spirit approached me, and I recognized her. She was someone I had known on earth. ...

"Marietta, we meet again. But," and she paused and gazed at me, "I know that you will not stay here, as I must do. **You can see that I am now a disembodied spirit. Everyone who inwardly denies the Savior comes here when they die.** ..." She paused, a look of pain spreading across her face.

"**Not only that, but your senses here are infinitely more acute. On earth there are many sins that do no more than give your conscience a twinge. But here, those same sins penetrate into the very essence of our existence, and the pain becomes a part of us. In addition to that, the awareness of suffering and the ability to suffer are far greater here than they are on earth.**"

Her face twisted in pain as she reflected. "God is just. He is good. We know this state we are in is not the result of a vindictive law of our Creator. **Marietta, this misery came about by our breaking the moral law.** We should have obeyed it, and then we would have been safe. We would have lived in peace and wholeness. ..."

"**But sin!**" she rasped, "**You parent of endless troubles!** You insidious enemy of peace and heaven! **Why do mortals love your ways?**"

Overcome by her feelings, she began to sob, and she did not speak to me again. Another spirit cried out, "**Go away and leave us to our lot. You just being here causes us pain. It reminds us of our lost opportunities and …** " He stopped and paused for a moment, then continued. "No, don't go. I don't know why, but I feel compelled to talk to you. I will tell you what we have learned here about the power of evil and why people are so attracted to it. Listen to me!" He paused again to gather his thoughts.

"**When a person is in the body, his spirit is difficult to perceive. It is inside him, invisible. But when he dies and enters this place, that spirit becomes the very basis of his existence. It becomes his whole being. It pervades everything, controls everything, and inspires everything. "People on earth refuse to believe that men and women will suffer for their sins when the spirit leaves the body. They think that the love and goodness of God would never allow this to happen. But evil and suffering certainly do exist in this place.**" …

He looked at me. "**Violation of God's law always has harmful consequences. It brings death instead of life and perfection. …**

It is sin that removes them from a life with God. "This fact is obvious in every aspect of our lives whenever laws are broken. This place is full of the awful results of it."

He lifted his contorted face and cried out in despair. **"Why don't people come to their senses and realize what happens when they sin? Why don't they stop sinning and turn to God to escape these terrible consequences?** We are overwhelmed by madness whenever there is even the mention of peace and love. ... **I am telling you these things because you are going back to earth. Tell those people what you have seen and warn them about the terrible things waiting for those who continue to gratify their wrong desires."**[8]

THE FAITHLESS

Instantly a vast arena opened up before me. At one glance I could see every imaginable kind of vice, together with every type of human society, government, and tribe. I saw atheists and every kind of religion as well as every form of worship. **Even the nominal churchgoing people were there, those who had worshiped under the message of the cross but with hearts untouched by it.**

---

8 Ibid., 41-56.

As I watched, I heard a voice from far above saying, **"Marietta, don't be afraid, but study this place of confusion. Here are the self-deceived, those who trust in false philosophy and those who hate God. You will also find the counterfeit Christianity of earth with religious mockery and hypocrisy. You will see human wolves who came dressed in sheep's clothing, which satisfied their greed by exploiting simple and unsuspecting people."**

As the voice spoke, a weird cacophony of sound fell on my ears. "Listen! Hear that wild chant! It is coming from the thousands who once sang hymns of worship to the living God without any feeling at all. Listen to that croaking organ. Look, the people are standing up. Watch what they do, and listen to what they are saying." …

As I looked, the choir in the galleries stood and began to sing. The dismal sound of the spectral organ grated on my ears, and note after note of their attempts at singing produced only mocking discords. I pitied them as I saw them sink back in utter despair. …

In a Gothic pulpit in front of them stood a man wearing priestly robes. He was their minister, but he had dishonored the Redeemer by his hypocrisy and pride. His love for God was a pretense, and his behavior had brought true Christian ministry into disrepute. In this dreadful place he represented all who

exploit and abuse religious things.

In front of him was an open book. He tried to read from it but failed at every attempt. ... He tried again and again but with the same result. His frustration increased until he burst out vehemently, cursing his own being and everyone around him. He then began to blaspheme God, blaming Him for every wrong and sorrow. He even tried to gather together all created intellect to curse the Creator of the universe. ...

But he suddenly gave up, exhausted, and I realized that his strength was limited, **and, to a large extent, he was under the control of his audience**. One glance at the crowd was enough to know why he was suffering like this. Their faces showed deep hatred and maniacal pleasure as they mocked his efforts. They reveled in fiendish delight at his dreadful agonies. ...

While he lay there, enveloped in the fires of his own unholy passions, one in his audience stood up and rebuked him.

"You fiend of darkness! **You child of hypocrisy! Deceiver! Unrivaled deceiver! You are in the hell reserved for the heartless religious teacher! You can never endure enough punishment! You turned religion and the souls of men into nothing more than a means of making a living. Yes, and for this you were even honored and respected! But you took things easy instead of reaching out to the souls of men and women. You did** not seek out ruined hearts, and you never brought them the soul-saving truth of heaven. All you did was tell them what they wanted to hear, and so you magnified their delusions. Now you are being tormented, and so you should be!"

"Get up, you false teacher in your silk gown! Get up and show us how great your false apostleship is. Speak smooth words to us, and lead the choir in their ludicrous travesty of a song." …

At this the minister tried to leave, but the speaker continued, "**No, you hypocrite! You want to escape, but you cannot. Look over this crowd of sufferers, and then ask yourself why they are here. Yes, it is true that each of them has sinned and is accountable for their actions. But can you look at them here with a clear conscience, knowing how you have misled them?**

"**Did you try to lead them to God? No! Instead you wrote learned essays and elaborate Bible expositions. You dressed your sermons with brilliant poetry and marvelous oratory, but the only result was that people were lulled into even greater apathy while you received honor for your clever words.**"

At this point the former minister cried out, "**Stop! Stop! Leave me alone! My remorse tortures me, and I have had enough!** … I know that all my life I did things just for pleasure. I trifled with men's souls and wrote about eternal things without any conviction. I put my prayers together only to please people. I interpreted the Bible to suit the selfish and fickle and proud, and I found excuses for those who oppressed others. … **My parishioners drive me mad with their bitter curses.** …"

As he said these things, the whole audience stood up and mocked him in his agony. The spirit who had rebuked him continued to censure him: **"You knew very well that we would have done what you told us to do. But when we did wrong things—things that could cause us to end up in this place— you, our supposed teacher of religion, did not try to correct us!** "The Bible, that sacred book, is a gift of God to guide people to heaven! But it was misinterpreted by ministers and theologians like you. You all loved pleasure; your hearts were far from God. Your version of the Bible was a passport to this place! "Now all we know is bitter grief. …"

"Do not curse your Maker," he laughed mockingly. **"This is your well-earned reward. Listen and I will quote you a Bible scripture that you so often preached so carelessly. Listen to this!**

"'The one who sows to please his sinful nature … will reap destruction.' (Gal. 6:8) Here is another: 'For the wages of sin is death.' (Rom. 6:23) "Those verses ring so loudly here now. They reach every home of every spirit. They touch every part of our senses. Worse still, they are magnified to the utmost by the doom of this place. "No, you false teacher, let God and His Word be true, for sin has done this to us. We suffer because we have violated God's law."

As he spoke these words, he began to tremble violently. He became more and more agitated until he and the rest of the congregation collapsed on the floor. As this happened, they seemed to lose their individualities and began to blend together into a mass of agitated life. Above this mass rose a thick cloud, so dense that it appeared to be a part of the writhing body below. The sight was too much for me. I could not endure any more of these woeful scenes.

I shrank back and cried, "Isn't there a God of mercy somewhere, and can't He see these things and save these people?"

"Yes," declared a voice above me. "**Yes, there is a God of mercy. He sees sinners and yearns for them with the greatest compassion.** Haven't you read the scripture that says: 'For God so loved the world that He gave His one and only Son, that whoever believes in Him shall not perish but have eternal life'?" (John 3:16)

The voice took on a grieving tone. **"But even though salvation is offered to the whole world, even though Christian believers explain it to sinners and plead with them, there are millions who refuse it. Then there are the millions of others ho** pretend to believe but have their own false ideas about redemption. Still others experience grief on earth because of their own sins, but many of these will not change. They fall into terrible misery simply because they broke the law of purity and love."

I looked up, trying to determine where the voice was coming from. "Don't be afraid, Marietta, but be aware of these things. Realize too that you have seen only a fraction of the suffering that sin brings to the spirits of men and women. Spiritual sufferings are beyond the power of description. Even the things you have just seen cannot give you a full understanding. Let me explain."

The voice continued. … **"In the pulpit you saw a false teacher and the bitter consequences of hypocrisy in religion. The people in front of him worshiped in the name of the cross but without a true reverence for God. They appeared to be worshiping, but their hearts were far away, trying only to please themselves in their devotions. They chose a teacher who wanted only to receive their accolades, so he tried to satisfy their every whim.**

"The spirit who berated him was one who trusted in false teachers and did not care about their own spiritual well-being. The conflict you saw is typical of this kind of people. Finally, Marietta, this scene demonstrated the verse that says, 'If a blind man leads a blind man, both will fall into a pit.' That is what happened here."

The voice paused and then continued solemnly, **"Marietta, you have had enough of these things, but do not forget them. Never forget that 'the wages of sin is death.'"** [9]

THE HEAVENLY MELODY

"Listen, Marietta," said the angel. With her right hand she pressed my temple, and from the deep silence I heard music begin. It was like angelic breath, like the inner and most holy life of the spirit. I could hardly hear it, yet it moved softly over and through me. I had never realized there were elements within me that could be awakened to such sacred music. I thought that my nature must have been totally transformed for me to experience such harmony. I felt totally at one with it.

As the sounds continued, it came into my mind to force myself into the music rather than simply allowing it to flow through me. My willpower wove itself into the sounds, and immediately discord flared up and the full force of my sinful nature swept over me. Note after note continued to penetrate

---

[9] Ibid., 62-70.

me, but they no longer moved in unison with the musical chords of my inner being. In striving to blend with the music, I had produced a terrible discord. Several cadences broke up in this way, and the music became harsh to me. I knew my nature could never meld with it.

The discord within me became agonizingly painful. Every part of me rasped and grated. The waves of harmony that moved throughout the dome foundered in a sea of turbulent sound when they fell into my degenerate heart. I wanted to get away. Any other thing or any other place would have been better by far. I thought even the hellish place of false worship would fit my nature better. But I could not escape.

I was completely disoriented. Each moment seemed like an eternity, and my condition became more and more awful. Finally I cried out in despair, "Let me get away from this place!"

I tried to analyze what was happening. I loved the sacred music when I first heard it. But when I tried to join myself to it, a discord was created and my unholy nature was exposed for all to see! Obviously I was not fit to be with angels. I was lost beyond redemption, my spirit broken and fallen. No part of it was compatible with that place. I cried out in agony, "Let me get away! Let me hide in darkness forever! Angel! Hide me! Hide me from this light! It has exposed my sinfulness! …

Is there a deeper hell somewhere? Let me go there—even if I am lost and demons mock me. At least my spirit would not be awakened only to be crushed because it is not fit for this place!"

So I pleaded to be released from the light and harmony and peace that filled that place. I realized I was completely unfit for paradise. **I had wanted so much to be there, but I had not considered what changes were needed in me before I could enter.**

…**when I was sucked down by the darkness, I had looked up to heaven, passionately wanting to go back there and be saved. Little did I know I could suffer so much agony from the love and harmony of heaven. I had no idea my own condition would cause me misery equal to the deepest hell.**

All these thoughts now raced through my mind as I begged for help. My condition was plain to me. I was certain all was lost and I was doomed to bitter grief.

At length the angel spoke. **"Marietta, you are not lost. Yes, your sin has been exposed, and you are suffering because your spirit has discovered its true state. But perhaps now you will understand how good God is in providing redemption and transformation through the Lord Jesus.**

"When you first came here, you had no idea of your real position. As a guest you were permitted to receive a covering

of holiness that protected you and enabled you to enter. But in this place, the breath of holiness is so perfect that your inner life was penetrated and your sin exposed. That is why you are suffering. "You can now see why God has arranged for spirits of similar nature to be kept together in the same place, with good and evil kept apart. The misery experienced by the evil is not increased, and the happiness of the good is not diminished. This is why the apostle John said that no unclean thing can enter the Holy City. For no unholy soul can ever enter this sacred temple or this city of inner life. In the same way, the inhabitants of this happy place could not live in the place of darkness with spirits that have not been reconciled to God."

The angel reached forward in earnestness. "**Marietta, can you see the goodness of God in this law of existence? It would be unjust of a righteous Creator if He condemned any of these infants to the dark regions. Their pure and tender natures would shudder if they were even touched by the inflamed passions of its inhabitants. Certainly God could be considered unjust if He treated the innocent in this way.**

"**In the same way it would be unmerciful to send an evil spirit to the place of holiness. For the greater the light and supreme good of that place, the greater would be their suffering.**"

She leaned back again. "**So, you can see that God is wise and good. This is the fulfillment of the Bible verse that says, …there is an impassable gulf fixed between the unholy and the righteous because the two extremes cannot blend." …

She paused for a moment and then spoke again. "**If mortals only realized this, they would war against evil and live righteous lives. Marietta, think about the things you have seen. Use your common sense and bring your life into order. Otherwise, a worse thing will happen to you, worse than just the realization that you are not fit for this place. When you return to the world, put your trust in Jesus. He is the only one who can make you fit to return so that you can enjoy the happiness here."**

The angel's rebuke struck my heart like an arrow, and I began to cry. "Do not weep, Marietta," the angel continued. "**A ransom has been provided to save your life. There is a 'healing fountain,' and it will wash away your impurity. So be encouraged! God's mercy is vast, and He offers redemption to everyone who wants to be rescued from their prison and brought into His kingdom. That is why the saints in heaven are always singing hymns of thanksgiving to their Redeemer. Day and night, they never stop!"**[10]

---

10 Ibid., 79-83.

⚜ Testimony of Marietta's Pastor

In the summer of 1848, a young woman named Marietta Davis, aged twenty-five years, residing with her mother Mrs. Nancy Davis, at Berlin, New York, fell into a sleep or trance, in which she remained for nine days. All endeavours on the part of her friends and of her physicians failed to arouse her from this unnatural state. When at last she awoke to a consciousness of external things, she was in the full possession of all her natural faculties, with an almost supernatural acuteness of perception superadded. Before she fell into the trance, her mind had been considerably exercised in regard to her future state; but there was yet a lingering doubt that greatly disturbed her. Her mother and sisters were exemplary members of a Baptist Church, in Berlin, then under my pastoral charge, but Marietta's doubt seemed to have kept her from the enjoyment of the hope in which her family so confidently rested.

But when she came out of the trance, in which she had lain for so many days, it was with joy and rejoicing over the unspeakable things that she had seen and heard. Her mouth was filled with praises to God, and her heart swelled with gratitude to him for his loving kindness. She averred that while her body lay as it were in death, her spirit had visited the eternal world.

She informed her friends that she was not to remain long with them: but should soon go hence to enjoy a mansion prepared for her in her heavenly Father's Kingdom.

After this she lived seven months and died at the time predicted by herself; and so perfectly did she know the hour of her departure, that when it arrived she selected a hymn and commenced singing it with the family; and while they sang, her spirit took its flight so gently as not to attract attention. Thus the hymn commenced with her friends on earth, and doubtless concluded with the angels in heaven.[11]

---

11 Ibid., 199.

3

Dr. Richard E. Eby

Dr. Richard E. Eby was a prestigious osteopathic physician and gynecologist, who graduated from Wheaton College and The Los Angeles College of Osteopathic Physicians and Surgeons. He was co-founder of the Park Avenue Hospital in Pomona, California, and served as the Executive Assistant of the American Osteopathic Association in Chicago. Yet, what he prided himself in more than his distinguished career, was the fact that he was a born again Christian. Let me introduce to you his testimony on his after-life experience.

"MIRACLE 29 - I NEVER GIVE UP

Time after time the Creator has used childbirth to teach a lesson about power, justice, or mercy. ... I shall never forget how

He handled a newborn problem early in practice. ...

It had been a long night for the mother and me. She was a fine, hardworking butcher at a meat market in town...the sun had just come up when her husky eight-pound boy finally arrived... The waiting family scurried to the phones to share their joy, as I changed clothes to drive to a neighboring town to deliver another mother there.

A half hour later the phone on the delivery room wall rang to notify me to rush back to Pomona; the new baby had suddenly stopped breathing just a minute before... I gasped, and ordered her to call the Resuscitator Squad from the Fire Department to work on the body until I could complete my work and drive back. ... Driving back seemed twice as far, and my watch revealed 50 minutes since the little boy had first stopped breathing. ...I burst through the nursery door... [and] I quickly checked for a sign of life. None at all. Already the little body was grey and cold, gone. ... The nurse turned away to hide a tear, and I laid my hand on the cold head.

'Dear Jesus,' I prayed, 'He was so loved down here! Won't you give him back to us? His mother needs him...'

I felt and heard the sudden cough at the same time! The body seemed to convulse. I opened my eyes and the nurse shouted 'Look!' ... The baby coughed and screamed. He turned pink and sharted shivering like he had just returned from a cold place. I could say nothing; just stand and enjoy the miracle of answered prayer. ...

The medical books say that eight minutes without breathing is fatal for infant brain tissue. Even partial anoxia can cause a 'vegetable' type of deterioration. En route home that evening I asked for one more miracle: 'Please, Jesus, give that baby a new brain undamaged and unhampered by these long minutes of death!' He did. Sixteen years later that local Progress-Bulletin carried the story of the fine football captain at Pomona High: he was 'our' baby—scholastically and physically a winner!"[12]

"MIRACLE 31 - IN MY FATHER'S HOUSE

In Chicago twenty days later I unexpectedly learned why my spirit had longed for a 60th birthday: God had been preparing me for the greatest gift He could wrap for me...

Maybelle [Eby's wife] has described for me the day's activities preceding my unscheduled visit to Paradise. ... We were busily sorting and packing into cartons various personal ef-

---

[12] Richard E. Eby, *Caught Up Into Paradise*, (Grand Rapids, MI: Spire Books, 1996) 187-189.

fects at the Chicago home of her departed aunt and late mother. My job was to load disposables from the second and third floors, and throw the cartons to the ground below the second storey wooden balcony. ... A hollow crunching sound suddenly froze Maybelle in her tracks. ... She dashed to the balcony, noted the missing railing, and gazed down in horror at my bloody, muddy body beside the broken sidewalk. The termite-eaten railing lay across the body. ... Her trance was broken by two ambulance attendants rushing past her to check the body. ... She noted that neither paramedic seemed in a hurry as they drove away toward the nearest trauma center hospital: no need to hurry with a d.o.a. aboard, she realized. Yet she was still believing for a miracle. 'God,' she implored, 'get down here right now. I need you. Don't let Dick die. I need him.' Her fists pounded wildly on the dashboard to emphasize her anguish. 'Please, lady, don't ruin our car,' implored the attendant as he tried to comfort her. ...

THE SIGHTS OF PARADISE

In the twinkling of an eye Jesus took me out of this world. ... My initial gasp ('Dick, you're dead') was as quickly followed by an overwhelming sense of Peace—peace which passeth earthly understanding—peace so complete that I instantly knew it was the promised gift of the Spirit from our Lord. … I was enjoying a heavenly 'body'; I was totally me… I looked like me, felt like me, reacted like me. I was me. I simply suddenly had shed the old body and was now living anew in this fantastic cloud-like body! Being a physician, my first instinct was to inspect my new body, and I instantly admired it! It was mine alright. After 60 years in the old one it was easy to see that the new body was me. I was the same size, the same shape, as the person I had seen in the mirror for years. I was clothed in a translucent flowing gown, pure white, but transparent to my gaze. In amazement I could see through my body and note the gorgeously white floweres behind and beneath me. …

Instantly the sense of timelessness made all hurry foolish, so I resumed my anatomy lesson, knowing that He would appear in His own time. … I instantly noted that my eyes were unlimited in range of vision; ten inches or ten miles—the focus was sharp and clear… There were no bones or vessels or organs. No blood. I noted the absence of genitals… Again my mind which worked here in heaven with electric-like speed answered my unspoken query: they are not needed; Jesus is the Life here. He is the needed energy. There was no air to breathe, no blood to pump, no food to digest nor eliminate.

This was not a carnal body of organs, mortal and temporary!

My gaze riveted upon the exquisite valley in which I found myself. Forests of symmetrical trees unlike anything on earth covered the foothills on each side. I could see each branch and 'leaf'—not a brown spot or dead leaf in the forest. ('No death there' includes the vegetation!) Each tree, tall and graceful, was a duplicate of the others: perfect, unblemished. ... The valley floor was gorgeous. Stately grasses, each blade perfect and erect, were interspersed with ultra-white, four petalled flowers on stems two feet tall, with a touch of gold at the centers. Each was totally alike! ... Having been an amateur botanist as a schoolboy, I immediately decided to pick a bouquet. To my amazement the unexpected happened. My thought (to stoop and pick flowers) became the act! Here in Paradise I discovered that there is no time lag between thought and act. ...

I found my hand containing a bouquet of identical blossoms. Their whiteness was exciting. I almost had time to ask myself 'why so white' when the answer was already given! 'On earth you saw only white light which combined the color spectrum of the sun. Here we have the light of the SON!' My excitement was too great to describe in words: of course, I thought, He is the light of the world ... in the new Heavens no sun or moon will be needed! Then I sensed a strange new feel to the stems—no moisture! I felt them carefully. Delicately smooth, yet nothing like earthly stems with their cellular watery content. Before I could ask, again I had an answer: earthly water is hydrogen and oxygen for temporary life support; here Jesus is the Living Water. In His presence nothing dies. No need for oxygen and hydrogen. I instinctively looked behind me where I had been standing on dozens of blooms. Not one was bent or bruised. Then I watched my feet as I walked a few more steps upon the grass and flowers; they stood upright inside my feet and legs! We simply passed through one another. …

The Sounds of Paradise

Just as was true of the light, the music emerged apparently from everything and every place. It had no beat…and had no tempo. (In eternity, how could it have 'time'?) …

The Perfume of Paradise

I was not prepared for the sweetest revelation of all: the all-pervading aroma of heaven. No one on earth, minister or Bible teacher, had mentioned to me this heady perfume! Like the sight and the sounds it was everywhere. … A perfume so exotic, so refreshing, so superior, that it was fit only for a King! … Earthly ingredients would fall short of perfection. I simply stood quietly and let it bathe my being. No answer was given my query about it in Paradise. This time Jesus waited till I was back on earth. 'Search the scriptures,' the Spirit advised me. 'In them you will find wisdom.' From Genesis and Leviticus through the books to Revelation He has told about His love of sweet smelling savors…"[13]

After Dr. Eby's experience in heaven, his spirit came back into his body and was shocked when he saw himself.

"MIRACLE 32 - MY PEACE I GIVE

I was shocked to find myself spread-eagled in Intensive Care with intravenous tubing and electrical wiring stuck in me here and there! I had no idea what had happened. I tried to move and found myself paralyzed from neck to hips. … Through the fog there materialized above me a two-headed face, out of focus, surmounting a Roman collar. I then realized that my eyeballs were at different levels and that my head was encased in a helmet-type bandage. As a doctor I knew what this meant: somehow my skull had split apart enough to shift the

---

[13] Eby, *Caught Up Into Paradise*, (1996) 198-207.

eyesockets; that would explain the lack of feeling and motion. But why was I alive? I summoned every ounce of energy to form some words: 'You must be a Father,' I whispered; 'What are you doing?' 'Yes, I am the Chaplain,' I heard him say. 'I am giving you the rites of the Church.' I could note his right hand shaking something over my limp body. ... I could see that he was very young, and quite frightened at hearing a voice from a 'dead man.' The two heads bent over me and he tried to laugh: 'You will live alright, I can see that,' he commented as the heads slowly shook in disbelief. 'Of course,' I murmured, 'I just came back from Heaven.' His face(s) turned white and he hurried from the room. ...

Suddenly the room lit up... out of the plaster where the ceiling met the walls was emerging the most gorgeously sculptured cloud of 'milk-glass' texture, self-illuminated! ... 'It' detached from the plaster and hung beautifully in space. then it spoke! And the voice was Jesus! Sovereign, regal, loving, authoritative, sweet, winsome, meek, powerful! All rolled in one.

'MY PEACE I GIVE UNTO YOU!'

'WITH YOUR HANDS YOU WILL HEAL.'

...I could see the Cloud receding majestically through the plaster, and realized that for those moments my eyesight had been 20/20. I looked back toward the nurse and fell asleep. He had given me His Peace! Another miracle."[14]

After this, Dr. Eby was completely healed and **currently only has a scar on his forehead to testify of the miracles he experienced.** It was 5 years after Dr. Eby visited heaven that he visited hell.

"For Maybelle and me it was a miracle just to be on this tour of Israel in April of 1977. ... Scarcely had we left Jerusalem behind and here was Bethany already; and up the hill was Lazarus' tomb. ... I ducked into the dark doorway and brushed away a tear to see better. ... A single bulb hung from the ceiling. ... I squeezed through the chiseled door-hold and stood up alongside two elderly ladies in an empty tomb .. Just then the Lord blew the fuse! The ladies screamed in the pitch blackness, and I reached out to reassure them, 'It's alright, ladies, the fuse simply blew.' ...

Then the miracle started... Suddenly the ladies were gone! ... In the twinkling of an eye Jesus was standing beside me! At

---

14 Eby, *Caught Up Into Paradise*, (1996) 209-212.

the same moment the tomb was filled with heavenly light. ... As I looked into His Powerful Face with those piercing eyes of love, I heard again that Wonderful Voice that had spoken to me from the Shekinah cloud in my hospital room five years before..."[15]

Dr. Eby told the latter half of this story in more detail in his other book, **Tell Them I Am Coming**.

"'My Son! ... I must show you hell, but just for two minutes! I have already shown you heaven. ...

You must tell them that I gave them a will when I created them.

They must make a choice between Me or My adversary, Satan. Man cannot live without a master; his soul is made to worship someone. Tell them I am a gentleman; I will never override their free will. I created them to be free to choose, because I would not create anyone to be a slave.

Satan offers them the security of slavery, but his wages are death.

I offer them freedom and the righteousness of My Father in

---

[15] Ibid., 225-228.

heaven, where our gift of love and life is eternal. ...

Tell them how much I love them!

I left heaven to come and die for them.

I had to destroy the works of the devil so My children could be freed!

I arose to present them blameless before My Father in heaven!

Tell them they can choose life with Me—all for free.

I paid the price.

Tell them they will have the unsearchable riches that My Father has prepared for them. They can choose to belong to the family of God.

They can reign with Me as kings and priests through the ages.

I will send them My Spirit.

I will heal their infirmities.

I will forgive their sins.

Tell them I took their place on My cross! ...

My grace is sufficient for them.

It is my gift of love.

They cannot earn it by their works.

I finished all the work and waiting on the cross.

All they must do is receive Me into their hearts and accept

me as their Way of Life!

Then we will be one! …

If they ignore or reject My love, if they turn away from My Father, if they refuse to listen to the urgings of the Spirit, there is nothing more that we can do for them.

They remain under the control of Satan, that liar and deceiver, for whom I had to create hell when he defied the Almighty God.

Because Jehovah is righteous, we had to punish Satan's wickedness and rebellion.

I never intended a human soul to go to hell;

[I]n fact I came down from heaven and died for mankind to redeem him from that deceiver.

I even went to hell and took the keys. …

There is yet a little while-but very little! …

I can't wait much longer; world events can no longer be postponed!" …

Suddenly, I was in hell! I knew I was trapped in the bowels of the earth. Instantly, I was in a stone, coffinlike cell, four feet wide and six and a half feet high. The terror was instantaneous and indescribable. … I tried to scream—no voice. … I looked down and saw clearly with the mind's eye of my fallen spirit-body many little, spiderlike demons about my feet. ... My mind told me that they were the 'chained demons' of Satan, and they agreed, saying, 'We are the chained demons, here to haunt and taunt you in hell! ... (Their actual language was so foul, it cannot be repeated.) You could have accepted God as your Father and Jesus as Saviour. We read the Book. You're trapped with us now, and Buddy, we'll make this your hell. Aha. Aha. You fool!' ...

I was suddenly snatched away and found myself standing before a gorgeous throne on which sat God... He was rapidly thumbing through a large book in His right hand. ... I found I had my voice again, and I heard it stammer:

'What are You looking for, God? My name must be there!'

'I am looking for your name in our family album, but I do not find it here,' He replied with a shake of His head.

'But it must be there, God! I lived a good life. I was never arrested or imprisoned. I obeyed the rules. I did good works. Look some more! ...'

'You rejected My Son's offer to be born again, to be washed

clean in His blood. Remember? You were told many times! There is nothing more I can do. You are not one of My children. You belong to Satan's family. ... Depart from Me into everlasting punishment with your father, the devil.'

In a split second I was back in the pit, and I slid like ooze among the little demons on the floor. Then I was snatched upward and found myself standing in Lazarus's tomb with the light on! My two minutes in hell without Jesus had ended! The guard was shouting to the three of us to come forth. 'No, the fuse did not blow,' he answered me. 'Perhaps something else? Who knows? The light failed here.' ...

I remember nothing of the other events of that day. For months I could not overcome the horror of hell enough to report its terror without sobbing... How can Jesus say it any more clearly than He did to me? 'Tell them. Tell them. Tell them.'" [16]

---

16 Richard E. Eby, *Tell Them I Am Coming*, (Santa Ana, CA: Fleming H. Revell Company, 1980) 30-36.

4

Jean Darnall's Mother

The following is an excerpt from Jean Darnall's exceptional book, *Heaven Here I Come*. It is the testimony of her mother's experience in the after-life.

We were family told by Christian friends that we should have a family altar in our home. The Pentecostal pastor explained that it was the place where we came together as a family to pray. It could be anywhere in the house. The main thing was that we met regularly to read the Bible and to pray together. So the kitchen table became the altar and after breakfast was the time. There we talked freely with one another and with God about everything.

AN UNUSAL MESSAGE GIVEN TO MOTHER

One Sunday morning we pushed back the empty coffee cups and waited before the Lord. **During the prayer time he showed something startling to my mother. She knew something unusual was going to happen that day which would drastically affect all three of us, but she didn't tell us.** It was good that she didn't tell us. We could not have accepted it as she did.

She tried to tell our pastor after the morning service. At the church door she asked if she could talk to him about something important. I was standing nearby as she stepped aside with him. "I want you to know what I'd like done about Jean…' Glancing towards me she stopped and asked me to go wait in the car. "Tell your dad that I'll be there in just a minute." She knew how impatient Dad would be to get home. He had a ravenous appetite since his lungs had been healed and he no longer smoked. He was anxious for his Sunday dinner; usually southern fried chicken, fluffy sour milk biscuits and country milk chicken gravy, green beans cooked with bacon and for dessert, hot apple pie.

"What's she talking so long about?" he asked after waiting five minutes.

"I don't know. She won't be long," I said, wondering myself

what it was all about. What was she asking the pastor to do about me?

Dad leaned on the horn. "She'd take all day if I didn't blow the horn," he said. Mother hurried out to the car. **Pastor Allan stood in the entrance of the church looking perplexed.**

She seemed anxious to get dinner over and excused herself to get aside to pray. The afternoon went by uneventfully. Soon we were off again to the church for the Sunday evening service. As soon as it was over Mother tried to have a few more minutes with the pastor, but he was busy and Dad was hungry again. So we went home.

MOTHER'S SUDDEN DEATH

While Dad raided the refrigerator for leftovers, Mother got ready for bed. Suddenly I felt a strong urge to go into her bedroom. Maybe she would like to talk about whatever it was that she had tried to tell Pastor Allan.

"Hi!" I poked my head around the door. "Mind if I come in?" Mother was in her nightgown, kneeling by her bed.

"Honey, come in and kneel and pray with me." She patted the chenille bedspread. I picked up a soft cushion and placed it on the linoleum floor close to her. We prayed together, united in our faith and concern for those we both loved. Then she stopped praying aloud. I waited. The room was very quiet. I decided she wanted to be alone, perhaps to pray about whatever had been on her mind all day. I tiptoed to the bedroom door. Glancing back before I shut the door, I was startled to see that she had slumped into a very unnatural position. She looked odd – slightly grotesque. I rushed back. "Mother!" I shook her. She fell limply against me. As I stepped back alarmed, she slipped down on the floor unconscious, or was she dead! She looked so strange; the vacant non-expression on her face.

"Dad, Dad," I shouted down the long narrow hall towards the kitchen. "Dad, come quick. Mother…she's unconscious. I think she's…She looks awful!"

Dad slammed the refrigerator door and came running. He helped me lift her on to the bed. We were so awkward. She was a big-boned woman, weighing over two hundred pounds. Her body was helplessly limp."

"Better go get Marie next door," Dad said with a tight voice. He was afraid. Before I reached the door he had started dialing the phone numbers of the doctor and the pastor.

"Marie's a registered nurse and she'll know just what to do," I thought as she and I rushed into the bedroom. I expected the nightmare to be over in a minute. Marie would examine Mother carefully and tell us not to worry…everything would be all right. She looked up and spoke softly to Dad, "Grace is gone, John." I gasped. Marie put her arms around me. "Jesus has taken your mother home to be with him, Jean." I pulled away and dropped to my knees, sobbing. She started to pull the sheet over mother's face. Dad fell across the bed, snatching it back. He softly slapped Mother's face. "Grace, Grace you can't go. Grace, wake up, wake up."

"Jesus," I cried out, "don't take my mother from me. Bring her back. Bring my mother back to me." I was in a corner with my face to the floor.

Marie answered the insistent ringing doorbell. Our pastor, the Rev. Allan, rushed in. "She's dead," Marie whispered.

"Mr. Murphy, come, get a hold of yourself–This is a great shock, but when a Christian dies it is a triumph, not a tragedy." Pastor Allan led my dad to a chair. Dad stared in disbelief at my mother. He said nothing.

Then Pastor Allan continued, speaking to all of us, **"This is one of the most unusual things I have ever seen happen in all my years of pastoring. Mrs. Murphy tried to tell me this morning that she knew she was going to go to be with the Lord today. She wanted me to know and she was concerned about what** would happen to both of you. Frankly, I could hardly believe what she was saying. It was so strange discussing funeral arrangements just like she knew for sure it was to happen today. She said the Lord had told her this morning during your family altar. Why, it is a marvelous thing. This is remarkable. I never saw a Christian die this way."

"No, no, I can't let her go," I wept. "We need her so." Anxiety flooded my mind. What would happen now? Would Dad go on serving the Lord? He depended so much upon Mother. How would I cope? I was fifteen years old. What would happen after I graduated from high school? These were unreasonable fears and my selfish heart would not let me listen to the reasonings of my pastor nor Marie. I prayed all the harder, "Oh please, Jesus, bring my mother back to me."

CAME BACK TO LIFE

Pastor Allan knelt beside me. "Jean, your faith is very strong. Don't use it to rob your mother of heaven now. She accepted God's will fully, can't you? She has God's perfect will. Don't force yourselves into something less than that." I prayed all the more. "I would not let her go. Bring my mother back to me," I cried out. My words echoed in the strange silence that followed. Minutes ticked by. No one seemed able to speak. We seemed to be waiting for something. I sat with my head buried in my hands. I didn't want to look up and see her there… looking so separated from us.

Dad's voice broke the silence. **"Look, look at her eyes."** He raised up out of the chair. We all looked. Her eyelids were fluttering, shattering the glassy stare. Then they closed. Had we seen her eyelids flutter or were we imagining it? **"Her lips are moving,"** Marie whispered. No sound, only a movement. Stunned, we watched. She slowly turned her head. She opened her eyes and looked at me. I felt she was looking at me form the other side of the grave. Softly, sadly, she spoke. **"Why did you bring me back?"** Her eyes closed again. I looked at Pastor Allan. I knew his word had been true. Dad still stared at Mother's face. Marie hurried over to take her pulse. The doorbell rang.

Dr. Brady rushed us out of the room, especially when he saw me kneeling by the bed, my face swollen from weeping. "Take her out of here," he told Dad. Marie stayed to help him examine Mother. "Mr. Murphy, come in," Dr. Brady called, out. Mother had suffered a major heart attack. It seemed to be ruptured and there were signs of a massive hemorrhage. "I must warn you," I overheard him say, "she may not last the night. I really don't understand how she has survived this long. I'll phone back every hour, and you phone sooner if you need me."

Each time he phoned, Dad would report that Mother was resting and her breathing was normal. Finally, about five a.m., the doctor phoned again. "How is she?" Dad said, "She is getting more rest than any of us. I'll call you if I need you."

For several days, Mother was reluctant to talk or eat. Mostly, she slept. When she was awake we could hardly interest her in anything. Gradually, she regained her strength and responded to what was going on around her.

THE HEAVEN MOTHER EXPERIENCED!

When she was able to walk, we led her into the living room to sit by the window. I drew up a footstool so I could sit close to her knee. **"Mother, what happened that night? Do you want to talk about it?"**

"Yes, honey, I'm ready now. You see, it started that Sunday morning. While I was praying I seemed to know without a doubt that I was going to be with the Lord that day."

I interrupted, "Didn't you feel sad? I mean, how could you think of leaving Dad and me? Didn't that worry you?"

"No, I didn't feel sad nor glad. It seemed so certain and final. I had no choice, so I accepted it. I was concerned about you. I seemed to know you'd be all right. I knew it was God's will. But I did try to talk to Pastor Allan about you. Remember when I stopped to talk at the church door after service?" I nodded. **"All day I expected it. Then, when you came in to pray with me, I felt the Lord was very near and He had sent you to be with me. As we prayed I saw Jesus. He walked into the room and came towards me saying, "Grace, I've come to take you home."**

"I didn't see him," I broke in.

"I know," Mother said.

Mother recalled how happy she had felt when she heard him speak her name. She was completely resigned to his will, she said. Then, he touched her head and she felt her spirit leave her body. "I was like a child again. I felt like a nine-year-old." She paused. "You know, that was the age l was when I first sought the Lord in that old-fashioned Methodist camp meeting."

She explained how weightless, unburdened and free she seemed after that transition. There were no tensions, anxieties, no pain, no weariness.

"I was a child standing by my Saviour. He held my hand. I

had a momentary glance at my old body slumped by the bed and I saw you kneeling there. In the next instant, the world was gone. Everything disappeared. We were standing in a different realm. It was strange and we were surrounded by darkness. The darkness extended as far as I could see, except where Jesus and I stood.

"How desolate it would have been if Jesus had not been there. At our feet was light. It was a thread of light extending upward as far as I could see. Jesus and I began to travel on this thread into the unknown, hand in hand, moving upward."

"How far, Mother? Did it seem a long way?"

"No, there wasn't any sense of time nor distance. It was another world, timeless, measureless, but not without direction. I definitely felt we were going up. We emerged into another environment. I can't explain it, too well. It was so different from anything we know here. I can only say what it was like. I'd compare it to a vast parkland; the most beautiful, restful, green park you can imagine. As far as I could see there extended this peaceful, restful scene of hills, soft as green velvet. They looked like they were carpeted, not with grass, but with some different element unknown to us."

I could see my Mother was finding it hard to explain her experience. "You rest a while. I'll get you a cup of coffee.

"Do you want to stop now?" I asked as I handed her the cup. I wondered if this attempt to describe her wonderful revelation was reducing it to a distorted image.

"**No, I want to share this with you, Jean. Then I don't want to ever talk about it again. It is too sacred. You may tell others whenever you feel it might glorify the Lord**, but don't ask me to. I don't feel I can, somehow."

As she sipped her coffee, I asked, "What else was there that was so different than things are here?"

"The music," she smiled. Her face was radiant just remembering it. "**The music was everywhere. I breathed it, like air. The atmosphere in that place was music. I was surrounded by it. I didn't see musicians, but sound seemed to take form in colour. Pastel colours blended and changed as the music varied in volume. It sounded similar to an orchestra and organ combined, and the moving colours were all one with it. It was above me, beneath me, moving through me.**"

"Were there no other people there?" I asked.

"Oh yes, everywhere."

"What were they doing? Sleeping?"

"Oh no, they were awake and moving around, but all seemed so relaxed and restful. Some were reclining."

She remembered the names of many whom she recognized.

She told me unusual names of people whom she had never known. I thought they sounded like Bible names. So I hurried to get the Bible with a proper name concordance. We found their names and texts in the Old and New Testaments that spoke of their faith in the Lord. I was surprised, since I knew that Mother had little Bible knowledge.

"Yes," she said, **"I knew everyone whether I had met them before or not."** Then, leaning forward, she took my hand and said, **"and the most wonderful thing of all is that I recognized my Mother."**

I gasped. How could that be true? Grandmother had died shortly after my Mother was born. There had been no way for her to remember her likeness. Yet, she described her features: the long black hair, the high cheekbones, the wide-set dark brown eyes. My grandmother was half American Indian and half Irish.

"It sounds like she had a strong Indian likeness," I said.

"Do you remember your cousin Leonard?" she asked. He was the one we called "the Indian" in our family because of his black hair and high cheekbones. **"Well, he looks a lot like your grandmother."**

"How can you be so sure, Mother?" I asked.

"I don't know, but I am as sure of that as I am that we are sit-

ting here. I know I saw my mother in heaven."

"How about your dad? You haven't mentioned him."

A strange look passed over her face. "No, and you know, until you asked me just now, I didn't realize that I didn't see him. There just didn't seem to be any memory of him at all. It's strange, I felt no loss at not seeing him there. Nothing." Mother leaned back and looked out of the window a moment.

"**Then, darling, as I stood there with Jesus, surrounded with the sights and sounds of heaven, I heard a voice penetrating it all. It was your voice.**" She turned to look at me. I remembered that night when she first opened her eyes and asked me, "Why did you bring me back?"

"**Your voice was clear, insistent. I heard you cry, "Oh. Jesus, bring my mother back to me." Jesus looked at me and said, "Grace, I will have to take you back." He took my hand and together we left that wonderful place, traveling down that thread of light. He let go of my hand and I felt myself settling into this tired body again.** It was strange how I became aware of my earthly surrounding in several definite stages of restoration. First, my hearing. I could hear you praying and weeping before I could see you or speak to you. Next I could open my eyes and finally, I could speak."

The music of heaven wafted into my mother's earthly consciousness several times afterwards. She would stop whatever she was doing and lift her head, enchanted, as she listened to music we could not hear.

"It seems like a breeze from another world brings it to me occasionally," she explained. **"You know, Jean, heaven is not very far away. It is only a different dimension. It is so near that if our eyes and ears were only touched by God we could see it and hear it right now."**

A SOLID EVIDENCE SUPPORTING HER TESTIMONY!

I wondered, was this experience a vision, a dream? Was my mother actually in Paradise with Jesus? Did she see her mother, really see her? She seemed so sure, even describing her resemblance to my cousin Leonard.

A few months later a tangible object was placed into our hands that established the reality of it all.

Mother had fully recovered. Her heart suffered no lasting damage. She was so well we were able to visit relatives in West Virginia. Far back in the mountains we visited the old family farm. My grandmother's elder sister lived there. Aunt Sis, as she was called, had been dying in regal style for several years. A tiny, frail figure, she was propped against enormous white pillows trimmed in wide hand-crocheted lace. She ruled from her four-postered throne of feather ticks and reigned over a large, grown-up family that waited on her hand and foot. She shook her head and wept as we told her how Christ had changed our lives, rejoicing that her prayers had been answered.

As we stood around the bed, she beckoned to one of the family to hand her some things out of the old trunk near the bed. She said to my mother, "Grace, here are some things that belonged to your mother. They were stored in this trunk before you were born. They should be yours. I want you to have them."

We all stretched to see. Out of the trunk came a stack of old-fashioned crochet work, delicate lace and embroidery. Mother began to sort out each piece, almost caressing them. **Her fingers touched something hard that slipped out from the folded fancy work. It was an old tintype photograph of a family. Mother pointed to a young woman in the group, exclaiming, "There's my mother. Yes, that is my mother!"**

"Grace," said Aunt Sis, amazed, "**how could you know that? She died while holding you to her breast three days after you were born. You couldn't remember what she looked like. As far as I know, that was the only picture ever taken of her. An** old traveling photographer, like a tinker, came along one day. I suppose she was only nineteen years old then."

Mother was staring at the photo. "I know her, for this is the beautiful girl I saw in heaven. Look Jean..." She held it up for me to see.

There she was, and she did look like Leonard.[17]

---

[17] Jean Darnall, *Heaven Here I come*, (Mukilteo, WA: WinePress Publishing, 1998) 42-51.

5

Elder-Deaconess Yeon-eui Nam

Next is a transcript of the recorded testimony of Elder-Deaconess' Yeon-eui Nam's after-life experience told by her daughter, Deaconess Yang-ja Kim.

THE FAITH OF A LITTLE GIRL

It was in the early 1900s that Elder-Deaconess Yeon-eui Nam was born as the eldest daughter of a Buddhist family. In the year she turned 12, Nam coincidentally met a missionary woman when she left the house that day with a servant and received Christ as her Lord and Savior. Although her family were well-known millionaires and sent their sons to Tokyo to study abroad, they had locked their daughter up at home. South Korea was a male dominated society at the time. That was why Nam spent most of her days stuck at home. Yet, a love for Jesus continued to grow fervently inside this young girl's heart each day.

When the elders of the family found out about this change, they tried everything from rebuking her to trying to persuade her. However, when Nam did not compromise and stayed firm in her beliefs, they persecuted her severely. At times, she was physically beaten, but whenever this happened, her faith only grew stronger. Yet, as time passed, Nam felt that she would become a living corpse if she continued to stay in a house that served evil spirits by bringing in the best shamans from all the provinces to perform exorcisms over 12 times in one year and by making terrifying idols made of straw to put in every grain storage. Thus, Nam made the decision to run away.

She started by coercing her mother, who loved Nam the most in the family. She persistently persuaded her mother that staying at home would end up killing Nam, so to instead let her leave to study diligently and make an honorable return. Nam's mother, who was secretly grieving for her little daughter undergoing such suffering, accepted her earnest plea. She helped Nam to disguise as a boy and sent her off in the middle of the night, with a backpack full of money.

THE GUIDANCE OF GOD AND THE TEST

So, Nam left her home, trusting in Jesus alone, but in reality, she had nowhere to go. However, God did not forsake this little girl, who believed and relied on Him, and gave her the impression to **"go to Daegu"**. However, because Nam had hardly left home before, even for errands, she had no idea where Daegu was or how to get there. But God impressed in her heart again that, **"Wherever your feet take you will be where Daegu is."** In this way, Nam walked for over a month and finally reached Daegu. Once there, she stopped an officer, and asked him, "I heard that there are many missionaries here in Daegu, can you show me where they live?" The officer then led her to a nearby western-style house.

There, an American missionary welcomed her warmly with a smile on his face. The missionaries, who had been about to start their early morning prayers, heard the request from the adorable child that she wanted to study here to grow her faith in Jesus. They took it as a sign that God sent her to them and with joy, they treated Nam as if she was an angel from heaven.

But shockingly, instead of educating her, the first thing they did was make Nam do all kinds of difficult household chores, such as doing the laundry, cleaning, and cooking simple western food. For Nam, who had never worked a day in her life, this labor was so intense and difficult, she wept sorrowfully by herself. Nevertheless, she overcame this hardship with the desperate passion of love for Jesus and her desire to study the Bible. Even while doing all the dirty and difficult chores, she did not lose her smile and continued serving with a joyful heart and sang praises.

Six months passed in this manner, and without one word of complaint, Nam continued to work diligently. One day, the missionaries called for her and said the following. **"Till now, we have been testing you to see whether you are a true daughter of God, whether you can truly become a precious worker of God, and whether you are capable of absolute obedience to God and able to endure it all. However, we couldn't help but be so impressed by you. All this time, you have done a great job of sacrificing and serving. So, starting from today, do not do any more laborious work and instead, we want you to learn and study the Bible."**

After saying this, they brought back their housekeeper, who had been sent away on vacation to test Nam, and from that day on, they treated her like a princess. Nam then started her first year at Daegu Shin-Myoung Girls' Middle School, which was operated by the missionary foundation during that time.

PERSECUTION FROM FAMILY AND MARRIAGE

With the wisdom God gave her, Nam was a model student who studied well and also faithfully followed Jesus. By the time she graduated five years later, Nam had transformed into a sophisticated, modern woman. She even earned a scholarship that would allow her to continue her studies at a theological seminary in Hawaii. During this time, it was very rare for a modern woman to be able to study abroad. So, Nam, being proud of herself, decided to visit home to receive the approval of her parents and make them happy.

Meanwhile in her hometown, Nam's family had believed their eldest daughter to be missing and had put out a handsome reward for those who knew of her whereabouts. Yet, with no progress, they had assumed she was dead and had given up.

When Nam arrived back home, transformed into a modern woman, the maid could not recognize her. When she revealed who she was, the maid finally recognized Nam and informed her family. Hearing this, her father and brother, who were playing Korean chess in the living room, came out with a bat. They said, "You first brought a western ghost and shamed the Nam Family and then ran away. Now, you have come back as a western ghost yourself, and since you have even entered our home, the Nam Family has now been completely ruined!" After making such a ruckus, they beat Nam relentlessly.

Nam fainted from the heavy beatings, and they locked her up in the attic in fear of rumors spreading in the town. Yet, because Nam's mother loved her daughter dearly, she nursed her by giving her special herbal medicine to help her recover.

After Nam's health was restored, she told her mother what had happened and her mother decided that there was no way to block the path of her daughter who was so devoted to the Lord. Once again, after signing all her documents to help her study abroad, Nam's mother helped her daughter escape.

That is how Nam was on track to leave for Hawaii on a military plane. However, when she was holding her farewell worship service on the harbor in Busan, Nam's brother chased after her and kept her from studying abroad. Once again, she was beaten and dragged home. Her family gave her an ultimatum: either she would be killed or would need to give everything up and get married. However, because Nam loved Jesus and made an oath to devote herself to the Lord, she believed that dying would be better than to be married into a Buddhist family. So, at her own risk, she carried out her third escape plan.

Nam could no longer even stay at the missionary residence in Daegu, so instead, she went to Shanghai, China. There in that foreign land, she only had the Lord to rely on, and once again Nam followed the guide of the Lord to the office of YMCA (back then, it really was the Young Men's Christian Association.) That is where she maintained her life of faith by associating with young Christians who were involved in the independence movement of Korea. During this time, the president of the group especially helped and favored her, and her heart opened up to him. The two eventually married as they believed they could fight together for the Lord. Nam was now 26 years old. Back then, women married at 12 and had children at 14. So, a 26-year-old would have been treated like a grandmother.

Nam's married life started back in Daegu. She had joined a well-known Christian household. However, her Mother-in-law was greatly disappointed in the fact that her eldest son, who she had even sent abroad to study, came back with a elderly bride. She was also worried that Nam would not be able to have kids. Furthermore, Nam was numerously persecuted for her modern woman image. Despite everything, the love of her father-in-law, a faithful Christian, gave her great comfort. Yet, the worry that Nam would not be able to have kids was for naught, as she had babies one after another. She had four children, but all of them were daughters. So, she continued to have another child, for the family wanted a son to carry on the family line. Unfortunately, the fifth and sixth child were also daughters. Nam then believed that her seventh would be a son. Devastatingly, it was once again a daughter. And the eighth daughter that came afterwards, is the very Deaconess Yang-ja Kim who compiled this testimony about herself and her mother.

Since she was young, Yang-ja Kim was saddened by the fact that she should not have been born. This sorrow turned into a deep scar. However, her wounded heart was healed after accepting the Lord through her mother, and she then felt proud to be the eighth daughter and was thankful. Thus, she was able to joyfully share the following story of when her parents prayed, holding her as an infant. At that moment, both of them received the same impression from God.

"Why do you not cry out to your living God when you have this desperate wish in your hearts? Till now, whenever you had a daughter, you simply gave thanks and said you would raise them wisely and beautifully. Thus, it could not be helped that this is the only request that was answered."

From that moment on, the couple prayed, with one accord, for a son to carry on their family line. Yet, this was when Nam was already forty-seven, and she had already had menopause. It was now impossible for her to conceive. Still, they held fast to the miracle that led Abraham, at the age of a hundred, and Sarah, at the age of ninety, to conceive Isaac. In the end, miraculously, Nam became pregnant. Not only was she blessed with a son for her ninth child, she also had another son to have a total of ten children.

THE DEVOUT FAITH OF YEON-EUI NAM

Yang-ja Kim heard her mother waking up every dawn to pray for her neighbors, who were alienated or in suffering, naming each person one by one and interceding for them. She prayed for each of her ten children and at the end of each prayer, she lifted up her tenth child as a tithe to the Lord and asked the Lord to use him as His servant.

Unfortunately, although Nam's faith was remarkable, her children's faith was not. Because they grew up in an affluent household, wishing for nothing, and received the best education, they were all prideful. And although they diligently attended church with their parents, who were well-known elders, and they even held positions as Sunday school teachers and members of the choir, they did not have sincere faith.

The youngest child, in particular, who was offered up to God to be a servant of the Lord as a tithe, grew up being treated as the emperor of the household, and started to drift away when he became a teenager. When he was younger, he thought being a servant of the Lord was the highest honor, for his mother constantly prayed it over him every day. But as he grew older, he realized this meant he needed to become a good for nothing pastor, and he started to rebel.

Even though her children broke her heart, Nam was not disappointed and continued to pray diligently. And because of her abundant love, she not only interceded for others, but actually sacrificed and served her neighbors without any boasting. When the sun set, she went out to the markets and felt compassion for the merchants who could not sell their products and she bought them for a higher price. She evangelized to them saying, "I am a grandma who believes in Jesus. I pray, you too, will believe in Jesus. God bless you!" Many souls were saved through Nam, for evangelism, based on practices of love, always moves others. Because her family was well-off, Nam took lettuce, potatoes and fish she had bought at the market, as well as excess clothes from her home and went to the slums and ghettos in the town of Hongjae. There, she gave away the clothes and food, saying, "Come take these goods, An old lady who believes in Jesus is here!"

There were many sick patients inside the slums. Most of them were those who had tuberculosis and vomiting blood, those waiting to die because of cancer, or those who were jobless due to malnutrition. Nam went into the reeking rooms of the patients and prayed for them while taking care of them. On days she evangelized like this, Nam returned home with swollen eyes from all her crying. She also carried home bags of infected ragged clothes, covered in germs, pus, and blood, and washed them to take back on her next trip.

However, her children persecuted her for all that she did, and they tore her heart into pieces by saying, **"Why do you have to believe in Jesus so pathetically?"**

"How ignorant do you have to be to evangelize only to people like this?"

"Why can't you be like our father and believe in Jesus in a reverent, holy, refined, gentlemanly, and intellectual manner?"

Meanwhile, Nam's husband, who was an elder, had a different attitude towards one's Christian life. His study was filled with different Christian scholarly texts, and he was so knowledgeable about the Bible that pastors would ask him questions and come to borrow his books. Moreover, because he was well off, he gave the most tithes and thanks offerings to the church and took the initiative in almsgiving. However, he delighted in these acts of showing himself off and boasting.

Because the children admired their father's attitude of faith more, they harassed Nam to be more like their father and yelled at her to stop embarrassing them and to stop going to the slums. Yet, despite being harassed by her kids and husband, Nam never fought back or lost her temper at them. She always answered them with a smile that God knows, or said they will understand when their faith deepens. All the while, she overcame her pain by crying and praying for them on her own.

THE DEATH SENTENCE AND THE GLORIOUS DEATH

Then one day, Nam, who had always been healthy with no illnesses, asked her youngest daughter to buy some medicine because she felt nauseous due to indigestion. But when the medicine did not work, Nam felt like something was truly wrong and asked to go to the hospital. Her children then realized the severity of the situation and brought her to the hospital. The doctor then diagnosed her with malignant, stage three, stomach cancer, and told her she was inoperable, with only 20 days to live.

When Nam's children realized their mother, who had been so healthy and just a few days ago had traveled all over the slums and was the evangelizing queen, had stomach cancer, they could not believe it. They firmly believed it to be a misdiagnosis and visited another doctor who was a cancer expert. Yet, the results were the same. Her ten children then brought her back home and mourned as they held a worship service for her.

However, something strange started to happen. Usually, the skin of cancer patients slowly darken to a charred color as they near death. Yet, Nam's face was the exact opposite and it started shining like the face of an angel and was gloriously transformed. She then told her ten children that when they neglected to praise, pray, and read the Bible, dark and wretched evil spirits in beastly shapes would climb over the fence of their home and enter the room, but that the evil spirits would be afraid and leave if they worshiped God. And so she asked them to continue to praise and pray and read the Bible by her bedside and to not stop. However, because it was impossible for her children, who had their own families to take care of, to be there 24/7, they decided to make a schedule. So, in three rotating groups, they stayed by her side. **During this time, the cancer patient's face shined brighter each day and everyone who visited her from their church were not only surprised, but rather comforted by her when they left.**

It was now September 23, 1968. Feeling a strange hunch, Nam called her entire family over and asked to have a farewell service and the room was overcome with a sea of tears. After the service, she requested her first and youngest daughter to remain and told them it was her time to go to the Lord and asked for their help to wash up and get dressed. She then asked them to dress her in a beautiful jade-colored Hanbok that she had prepared long ago for this day. When the preparation was over, she once again gathered her family together and told them her three final wishes and pleaded with them to keep it.

First, she asked them to, above all, be filled with love and follow after the ultimate love of the redemption of the Lord and to practice this love. Although she tried her best to act out this love, she was unable to finish doing so and earnestly asked her children to practice it in her stead.

Second, she strongly urged them to keep a diligent tithing life. She told them they need to return one-tenth of their earnings for the work of God, as He allowed them to use nine-tenths when actually, all things belong to God. If they stole even that from Him, they would never be able to receive blessings.

Third, she told them to become a believer that is the wheat and not the chaff, be dedicated to the church, and serve the servants of the Lord faithfully.

After saying her final wishes, Nam made her ten children repeat it three times and was finally at ease. Then, she joyfully told them, **"These are not my words, but the commandments of the Lord. So, till the day you die you must keep them well so that we can all meet in heaven."** At last, she lifted up her frail arms and looked up to heaven, with her spiritual eyes opened, and said, **"O God of love, I thank you for your great grace. You are now calling me to you, so I will go to be by your side."** And her spirit slowly left her. Immediately, the room erupted in tears and the wailing sounds of her children cried out, "Mother, mother, our poor mother! We were never able to give you luxuries and you left, having only suffered! We are undutiful children, forgive us!"

THE SHOCKING TESTIMONY OF YEON-EUI NAM, WHO WAS BROUGHT BACK TO LIFE

As time passed, everyone had grown weary, and they left to

go prepare for the funeral. However, Yang-ja Kim remained and continued to pray as she beat her chest and rolled around crying.

"Oh Father God, I believe you are alive and working. Please have pity on my mother. If you save her, I will give my life to dutifully serve her!"

She cried out like this while embracing her mother, rubbing her cheeks on her and was near-hysterical. Kim thought she was alone, but she then realized that the youngest was also next to her, crying desperately and without abandon. Nam had prayed for him to be a servant of the Lord, but he rejected this prayer as he grew up and strayed from the path, which broke his mother's heart. He wept bitterly as he embraced his mother. Then, he grew weary and left the room.

Now, Yang-ja Kim really was alone and she cried with all the more yearning. Five hours passed by, just like that. And when she felt like if she cried any longer she would go mad, she suppressed her sadness and fixed up her mother's body and cleaned and covered her up with a sheet. And on the way out of the room, she looked back once more.

In that very moment, Kim stood, shocked out of her mind.

She doubted what she was seeing with her eyes because, lo and behold, her mother started to move underneath the sheet! At first, Kim thought she was hallucinating but as she came to her senses and looked again, she was sure this was actually happening. So, she screamed loudly, **"Mother is alive!"**

When her family heard this, they thought she had gone crazy from crying and rolling on the ground for so many hours. Kim thought they didn't hear her and she yelled again, louder this time. When she did so, the youngest came running and by then, Nam had already put aside the sheet that was over her and was rolling her eyes around.

When the youngest also yelled, **"Mother is alive!"**, all were surprised and came tumbling into the room. And they all stood there, frozen in place. Yang-ja Kim was the first to run to her mother, and she hugged her while crying tears of joy. However, Nam's eyes were not yet focused and she looked around the room and could not recognize anyone. She asked nonsensically, **"Where am I? Why am I in this place? I'm not someone who should be in such a dirty, awful, and foul-smelling place…"** Feeling sorry for her mother's strange words and actions, Kim shook her and spoke loudly, "Mother, wake up! Can't you see where you are? What do you mean it's dirty, awful, and foul-smelling and rotten here? This is your house and your room, please wake up!"

That is when Nam's eyes settled from looking around the room, her eyes started to focus and she was able to look at her daughter properly. Then, her eyes started to shine brightly. Moreover, her feeble voice, which you could barely hear five hours ago, suddenly changed into a loud and authoritative voice when she opened her mouth to speak.

After Nam recognized her family, she called their names and said, **"My children, listen carefully. There is not much time. Hurry and call our families and relatives. Tell them I have something urgent to say."** Everyone was overpowered by her beaming eyes and her confident voice that they ran out the door saying, **"Yes, we will do it right away!"**

Nam's family divided into three teams to make this happen. The first team ran to the payphone at the local bus stop. The second group went to wake up their next door neighbor to borrow their telephone. The rest opened up the phonebook and started calling all their relatives. Nam had come back to life around 11:30 p.m., so there was only 30 minutes left before the official city-wide curfew began. It looked like it would be an impossible task to call and gather her relatives who lived all over Seoul.

Yet, a miracle happened. Even though it was so late, and

there was no reasonable explanation for how and what they rode to arrive at the house, everyone arrived before the curfew began. Nam asked to be moved to the middle of the living room and to even open the doors of all the adjacent rooms so they could have plenty of space to be around her. Her ten children stood chronologically next to her, but there were over 40 people in the house. Then, Nam opened her mouth and started to speak.

"My beloved ten children, my husband, and all my relatives, what I am about to say are not my words, but direct words from the Lord. So, please listen carefully and do exactly as He says."

She spoke as if she was a powerful prophetess. Her voice was authoritative, strong, and confident and her eyes radiated so brightly that everyone was completely overwhelmed.

From this point on is that testimony of heaven and hell told by Elder-Deaconess Nam.

The Hell Nam Witnessed!
When Nam left this world, she saw the heavens open and a beautiful cloud of flowers come down in front of her home.

The archangel and six other angels guided her spirit onto the cloud of flowers, and they departed. She was deeply moved and grateful for the grace of God, sending her the cloud of flowers with angels. Yet, at the same time, she was terribly ashamed it was being given to a sinner like her that she wept on her knees.

Then, she saw that the other angels, apart from the archangel, were all young and beautiful. Yet, what was more amazing was that **Nam, the 70-year-old cancer patient who was gray-haired, suddenly found herself transformed into a beautiful and young spiritual being.** Philippians 3:20-21 says, "But our citizenship is in heaven, and from it we await a Savior, the Lord Jesus Christ, who will transform our lowly body to be like his glorious body, by the power that enables him even to subject all things to himself." And just like this message, Nam saw her lowly body transform into a glorious body, and she knew that not one iota of the Bible was false and that it is certainly the truth. Filled with this joy, she continued to ascend, but then she saw something terrible revealed before her eyes. **With a special purpose, God showed Nam the world of hell.**

Suddenly, she heard someone calling from behind her saying, "Mrs. Nam, Mrs. Nam!" Next, she heard, **"Sister Nam, Sister Nam!"** She also heard the sweet voice of her childhood friend who she was close to. **Nam thought to herself, 'How strange! What is this sound?'** But when she turned around, she was terribly shocked.

While standing on a cloud of flowers, she looked down, deep below. That was when she saw something like a dark pit, or a basement, or the deepest depths of a dark cave. This place had burning sulfur that was boiling up from a thousand meters down, and the raging fire went up high and down low like the waves of the Pacific Ocean soaring up high and crashing down again. The fire of sulfur was so terrifying that Nam almost fainted. That is when she realized the call of her name was coming from within. "Mrs. Nam, Mrs. Nam!" Others called out, "Sister Nam, sister Nam!" or "Yeon-eui, Yeon-eui!" Nam wanted to hear what they had to say, so she listened carefully and this is what she heard shouted at her.

"I can't stand one more second in here, I am dying from this burning sulfur and in the worst possible pain. Even though I want to rest, I am not able to. I want to lie down but cannot lie down. I want to sleep but cannot sleep. It doesn't stop for even a second, and I have to stand in this fire, constantly burning. I can't stand this. It's too hot. It's too painful. I can't stand it."

And as they enviously watched Nam, who was going up to heaven on a cloud of flowers, they howled in the fire, "Elder Nam, Elder Nam, Save us! Deliver us from this burning fire! Save us!"

Nam came back to her senses and when she looked to see who they were, she was extremely shocked. **"Oh my dear friends! Oh my dear sisters! What happened to you, why are you in hell?"** She was truly shocked. A fellow Elder, who was considered one of the most devout Christians, had passed away not long ago. Nam had thought she would be in heaven, waiting for Nam to join, but instead, she was waving her hands in a burning fire in hell. She implored and cried out, **"Elder Nam, Elder Nam, I cannot bear this heat, but there is no way out of this pain. It's not something that will end soon, and I will be living forever inside this fiery pit and it's too unbearable. Elder Nam, please, please, when you go to heaven, tell them that I, an Elder-Deaconess, am lost in this place."**

It took some time to collect herself after hearing the above, but when she did, Nam looked down again and she saw blackened and charred figures, bouncing around inside the lake of fire. Once again, she was surprised when she focused on them. For these objects that looked like pieces of wood that were burnt and floating in the lake of fire, a meter apart from one another, were actually people. Their eyes, nose, mouth, and feet had already all melted in the fire and were gone. They became these charred figures existing inside the fire, but their souls cried out to Nam. And Nam was able to recognize some of them.

"Oh, my dear friends, oh my dear sisters, oh my dear Pastor, what happened to you that you are here?"

Yes, there were pastors in hell too. There were pastors, elders, and numerous believers who served the church that were in the fires of hell. Nam was extremely shocked. But after seeing this, she realized that God's perspective and man's perspective are completely different. God, with fiery eyes, sees the center of our hearts. And God certainly judges those who seek Jesus only outwardly, who aimlessly go back and forth from church, and even those who seemingly give generous offerings and involve themselves in plentiful almsgivings, if they are actually wicked at heart, disobedient, and living a rubbish Christian life.

Even after realizing all this, out of compassion, Nam stretched out her hand. She had pity on them and wanted to take them up on the cloud and save them. She called out to one of them, "Sister, hold on to my hand." At that moment, the archangel tapped on Nam's shoulder and said the following.

"Elder Nam, you have been consecrated and set apart from those people, so do not look at them or speak to them."

In that moment, hell suddenly grew further away. Nam then knelt down and bursted into tears saying, "Lord, I am a sinner, and I am the foremost of all sinners. I lack faith even more than those people, so why are you not sending a person like me to hell and instead, bringing me to heaven?" Considering herself a sinner who deserved to fall in hell, Nam fell down weeping, overwhelmed by this amazing grace. As she wept, the archangel tapped on her shoulder again and said, "You are now heading towards heaven to meet the Lord, and God is pleased when you give Him glory and praise. So, let us sing praises together." Nam thus stopped weeping and held the angels' hands. She and the angels started to praise God and danced with overflowing joy.

After much time had passed, the cloud of flowers finally reached a grandiose and massive white marble door. As she was about to walk through, Nam thought to herself, 'Behind this door is heaven!' Yet, all of a sudden, she shuddered and was seized by the worst sort of fear. 'How strange! If this is heaven, it should be overflowing with joy, peace, and overwhelming bliss but...' Her thoughts were stopped midway as she realized that **God, with a particular purpose, was now showing her the judgment seat.**

There were many souls waiting in two long lines, and they were all overtaken by terror and shuddering like a leaf. Moreover, their eyes were full of uneasiness and anxiety and they seemed to be restless. When their names were called, they faced the judgment seat and their lives flashed before them like on a movie screen. Then, the last judgment was pronounced. They looked absolutely dreadful while they waited their turn, trembling in fear. It even seemed that burning in the sulfuric fires of hell might have been preferable to going through this process. In this place as well, Nam saw souls that she knew, and they begged her to put in a good word to Jesus for them. But because their fates were already sealed, there were no allowances for compassion. Nam was so shocked by this situation that she forgot the joy of entering heaven and continued to cry instead.

The Heaven Nam Witnessed!

But while she was crying, Nam saw a light shine upon her that was so bright, she could not open her eyes. When she asked the archangel what this surrounding light was, he informed her it was because she had reached heaven. The first thing she noticed, when she stepped into heaven, was the beautiful fragrance that mesmerized her. And as she stood smelling this beautiful scent, wondering where it came from, all her past sadnesses and shock disappeared. She felt herself overflowing with joy and peace. Then, Nam saw the endless fields of flowers around her. There were many flowers here that could not be found on earth. Nam had always loved flowers, so she had planted many of them in her yard and had even asked to have flowers planted around her grave. These beautiful flowers in heaven responded to one another with songs praising God.

As they did so, she heard the praise of a choir and saw hundreds of cherub angels come before her and welcome her. Their beautiful singing completely captivated Nam. And this beautiful singing was heard throughout heaven, wherever she was. They continued to walk into heaven, with the archangel in the front, then the cherub angels, then Nam, and finally the six angels walked behind her. Surprisingly, they weren't walking at all, but were rather a meter off the ground, floating in the air. Even when Nam tried to ground her feet, she stayed in the air and was left in awe.

They walked like this for a while into heaven, and then everyone left except for the archangel. He pointed far up ahead and told Nam that Jesus, her bridegroom, was waiting for her, His bride. Finally, this was what Nam had been waiting for her whole life! This was why she withstood all the persecution and ridicule and why she fought the good fight. It was for this one person, for Jesus, and the fact that she was about to meet Him overwhelmed her, and she froze in her spot.

Jesus stood far off, shining in light, standing in a shimmering white gown with both arms wide open. Yet, because Nam could not dare lift her face to see Jesus and could not confidently walk towards Him, she covered her face with her hands and crawled to Him. She cried tears of joy as she took her time crawling to him, until she kneeled at the feet of Jesus.

Then, she heard the voice of Jesus say, "My beloved daughter Yeon-eui." However, she still could not dare to lift her face and continued to prostrate herself in front of him. Once again, she heard Jesus say, "My beloved daughter Yeon-eui." Still, she did not have the courage to look. That's when Nam heard a voice in her heart, 'You fool, did you not live your entire life for this one moment? Next time He calls you, be brave and stand up and go into His arms."

For the third time, Nam heard Jesus' voice call to her. Immediately, she jumped up and said, "Lord, here I am." And she looked into the eyes of Jesus. Yet, the moment her eyes caught

His, she yelled out, "O Lord, I am a sinner!" and she embraced herself with both arms and fainted. For the face of Jesus she expected to see was one that was patient and merciful and full of love. Yet, in reality, He was stern-looking, and his eyes were filled with fire that saw through all and like a clear crystal, all her disgusting sin was exposed in front of her. That was why Nam tried to hide herself with her two arms and fainted.

With a trembling and fearful heart, she cried out beating her chest in repentance, "O Lord, It was wrong of me to think that a sinner like myself could enter heaven. Forgive this sinner!" While she was deep in her tears of repentance, she heard the voice of the Lord repeat three times, "My beloved daughter Yeon-eui." Nam replied saying, "Lord, here I am, a sinner," and she stood up on wobbly legs and looked to the Lord. However, this time, the face of Jesus was full of love, patience, and mercy, and He stood there with a soft smile on His face. Then, he opened His arms wide open and embraced her. The warmth of His embrace was so soft, so comforting, and so beautiful that she dug deeper into that embrace, as strongly as she could. Jesus patted her on the back and said, "My beloved daughter Yeon-eui, you have suffered so much till now." Nam was so moved by this that she started to wail.

Nam stayed in Jesus' embrace for a while. During this time,

another visitor came to see her. It was her father-in-law, Elder Kim. He embraced his daughter-in-law with open arms. Elder Kim was a very faithful Christian, enough to be nicknamed Grandpa Jesus. He planted a church in Daegu and lived in a town of lepers for all his life. He gave everything he could eat or wear to serve the lepers and he lived his entire life with just the clothes on his back. He was one who personally practiced the love and sacrifice of Jesus. Thus, Elder Kim was highly esteemed in heaven.

This esteemed man embraced Nam and said, "My beloved child, my beloved daughter-in-law, come here and give me a hug." Nam was so excited to see her father-in-law that she leaped into his embrace and rubbed her cheeks against him. Their reunion in heaven was extremely overwhelming and touching because she had missed him so much that she did not stop weeping for months when he passed away. Then, Elder Kim told her, "I knew you would come and have been preparing the way for you," and they shared many things that had happened to one another.

But while Nam was talking with him, the archangel came to her and said, "There is no time for this. Jesus is calling for you again." Nam then came to her senses and followed the archangel until she was standing back in front of Jesus. Then, Jesus spoke solemnly to her.

"My beloved daughter, listen carefully. You believe that you are in heaven right now and are rejoicing, but your call is not over yet. Do you think you have the right to enter heaven when you have not finished your duty as an elder? As a servant of love, yes, you have achieved much. I know that you have even won the evangelizing award three times and are called the queen of evangelism. However, you have not done what is the bare minimum of your call. You have not been able to save your flesh and blood and thus, your other accolades have no worth in heaven. Not a single one of your ten children have become a true Christian, so how could you say that you have fulfilled your call and try to enter heaven? That is not possible. So hurry, go back to the world, and go to your children, families, and relatives, and fulfill your call to save them. That is how you will earn the right to enter heaven and that is when I will call you again."

When Nam heard all this, she surrendered herself to the Lord and cried out the following confession. **"Your words are true Lord. It was wrong of me to think I could enter heaven when none of my children are saved. I left my children to the** world and did not keep your commandments and I broke your heart. Lord, forgive me. Now that I know my call, allow me to go back to fulfill it." In that very moment, Nam was lifted up onto the cloud of flowers by the angels and swiftly traveled down to earth and arrived in front of her home.

This is when Nam's body started to move under the covers. And because she had just spent time in heaven, where it was filled with beautiful fragrances, the world on earth seemed so dirty and wretched in comparison. The human world smelled rotten, filled with the worst cesspools of sin. It was only after going to heaven that she realized humans are no better than insects living in this place. That is why when Nam opened her eyes she asked where she was and spoke nonsense and why her children could not understand her.

THE SPIRIT OF REPENTANCE STRIKES THE WHOLE FAMILY

While Nam testified of her death and coming back to life to her family, an amazing miracle started to occur. The gathered forty relatives started breaking down and they started to believe that God is alive and working even today. They believed in the existence of heaven and hell, even though they used to doubt it.

And they believed in the message of Hebrews 9:27 that "just as it is appointed for man to die once, and after that comes judgment."

Just like how there was an amazing work of the Holy Spirit in Mark's Upper Room, the Holy Spirit worked powerfully in Nam's house. It was like a modern reimagining of Mark's Upper Room. Most of the Kim Household who were gathered there, were those who had the best education. Some were even educated in America, and others had doctorate degrees. All of them were wealthy and some were even conglomerates or high officials in the government. Thus, they were all consistently prideful. Even though they grew up in a Christian household, they were worldly and corrupt like Judas Iscariot, who sold Jesus for 30 pieces of silver.

In the past, whenever Nam had time to visit her ten children and relatives, she took the time to individually persuade them to repent and return to Christ. Sometimes she visited their offices and pleaded with them in tears, but they in turn scorned her and ridiculed her for embarrassing and pestering them and turned her away. Nevertheless, Nam did not give up, even until all her hair turned gray. Thus, it was this grandmother who had died and come back to life and testified of heaven to them. She called each person by name and rebuked them saying, "Repent!" And that is why the Spirit of repentance fell upon the place and the house became a sea of tears. It was not only her ten children, but all her relatives who lifted up their hands with trembling. Some could not stand still and were rolling on the ground in agony as they repented. Others ripped their shirts and ripped at their hearts to the point of seeing blood. Another person hit their head so hard on the wall that it caused an aneurism. Another person ripped out their hair and lost two fistfuls. That was how desperate they all were.

They cried out, **"Living God, forgive me of my sins. I had no idea you were alive God. I didn't know that you were watching each one of us with fire in your eyes. Nor did I know the truth that you would judge all of us and separate us into heaven or hell. Lord, forgive me of the sin of selling you like Judas Iscariot did for money and the pleasures of the world and of the sin of nailing you on the cross."**

All of them threw away their pride that day and were weeping and wailing. They were like young children as they innocently opened up to reveal all of themselves. As they repented, God accepted them all as His sons and daughters and poured out the Spirit upon them. That was how each of the 40 people in that house repented and received the Lord.

When Nam completed her calling in that room, her spirit once again returned to heaven. Through Elder Nam, God's servant of love, her ten children and their families, who were false believers, fake believers, sham believers, and empty-husks, were convicted of their sin, and received the grace to be upright before the Lord. They became true believers and witnesses to testify of heaven and hell, as well as valuable workers who inherited the gifts of love and evangelism like their mother. Moreover, the youngest son, who Nam had previously lifted up to the Lord as a tithe offering, decided to give himself to the Lord because of his mother's testimony, and he became a powerful pastor.

Deaconess Yang-ja Kim, who lived in New York, preached the kingdom gospel all across America and even at foreign conferences. Through her powerful testimony that caused people to weep, Kim helped countless souls repent and receive salvation. Her sister Jong-wook Kim, who also lived in America, visited nursing homes and the elderly who did not have much time to live. She too, through testimonies and the kingdom gospel, saved countless souls until the day she died. Like her mother Elder Nam, she did so by showing her love through actions and service and was well-known by the locals as the

"Little Angel." Not only this, but the rest of Nam's children and relatives all became precious children of the Lord as they quietly fulfilled their duties in the church, were faithful even with small tasks, and as they served the servants of the Lord. Praise God![18]

---

[18] Yang-ja Kim, *Oh, My Beloveds, Oh My Dear Pastor and Saints, What Happened to You That You Are in Hell?* (in Korean), (Seoul, South Korea: HolyPearl, 2022) 7-43.

6

Pastor Bob Jones

The next excerpt is from Pastor Bob Jones, who is known as "the living legend" or "the father of prophets." It is a transcript of the testimony he shared, per my request, when he came to hold a special conference at our church.

Last night an evil spirit visited me. The evil spirit told me, **"Don't share God's message. Don't share what you are going to share."** The message that I am about to share troubles me. But the more Satan disturbs me, I am more confident that the Holy Spirit wants me to share the message to you.

Many years ago the Lord took me to heaven. He showed me many things. Then He took me to hell and showed me hell. Hell is real. There is no word in this world that can properly describe hell. **After seeing hell I was physically sick for many days.**[19]

HEAVEN EXPERIENCED THROUGH 5 SENSES

First, I will tell you what I saw in **heaven**. Human beings have five senses. You see, hear, smell, taste, and feel. When the Lord took me to heaven, I heard music of all kinds.

Also in heaven are many beautiful trees. Trees like pine trees blowing in the wind. But this wind sang praises to God. It was so beautiful. I also saw birds that sang, birds that sang praises. In many cases birds come down to earth and remain among the children of God who praise Him. They give songs of praises spontaneously to people. You can expect more of these things to happen. I also saw flowing water. They were singing praises. Everything in heaven was singing praises to God. I also saw angels flying in the air. Angels sing praises unto God. Every angel was singing praises. These were the most beautiful songs—songs I've never heard before. **I did not ever want to leave that place.** But I had to go up to the next level and leave that place.

In the next level, my eyes beheld a beauty. Everything I saw

---

[19] Bob Jones, *You Are My Friend*, (Seoul, South Korea: HolyPearl, 2009) 66.

was so beautiful. There were houses and they were made with precious stones. Every precious stone used for houses reflected something. The stones reflected one person. That Person was Jesus.

In heaven, there were mountains, and these mountains were so beautiful. They were beautiful beyond words. So I was looking at the mountains and I was thinking I wanted to climb to the top. The moment I had the desire I was immediately at the top of the mountains. There I saw a large lake. The lake was so beautiful and its color was blue. I thought, "Do fish live up here?" The next thing I saw was the bottom of the lake. And there I saw every kind of fish. It was beautiful. Everything I saw there was beautiful. Everything that exists on earth is a shadow of the things in heaven.

On earth there are seven colors. A rainbow has seven colors. In heaven there are many different kinds of colors. Perhaps there were over 700. Everything I saw there was so beautiful. There I saw grass, and as I was lying there I watched one blade of grass. As I was watching this, I was amazed. No matter how much I looked at that blade of grass, its greatness was beyond understanding and amazement. It was so green and beautiful. Afterwards I saw how one blade of grass grew and it was a miraculous process.

Everything I saw with my eyes was so beautiful. There were streets in heaven. The streets looked like marble, but also like glass. There were streets of gold. They were so transparent that your reflections could be seen. I could see the beauty within you reflected in the streets. There I saw beauty that could not be seen on earth. All the houses there had flat roofs and were made of gold. Everything there reflected the glory of God.

The next thing that happened was the beautiful smell of flowers. The fragrance gave off its smell by the wind. The fragrance was like honey and roses. The flowers had such a beautiful smell. These fragrances flowed over like water. **Even with eyes and ears closed, I could spend eternity there just with smell.** It was an amazing place. When I said I was thirsty, an angel came with a cup of water. It tasted more fresh and delicious than any water I've tasted before. It was so refreshing and tasteful. I could taste what happiness felt like through that cup of water. It was a living water that came into my body.

There were fruits in heaven. There were peaches that were more beautiful than any peach I've seen on earth. The peaches in heaven were as big as a watermelon. I asked the angel standing next to me to give me a peach, and asked if I could taste it. The angel said I could. I took hold of a peach and took a bite. The juice that I tasted from that peach was something

I'd never tasted before. It was so sweet to my taste. There were many different kinds of fruit in heaven. Each fruit had its own taste that was beyond anything you've tasted on earth. The moment I took one fruit from the tree, another fruit grew in its place. The taste of the fruits there were incomparable to the taste on earth.

The fifth thing that happened to me was, **I closed my eyes, ears, nose, and mouth. I concentrated on the feeling. Then I felt deeply loved and a feeling of happiness covered me. It was as if I was in a cocoon of love. The feeling in heaven is a complete feeling of love. Complete security. It was full of glory inexpressible. Everything you feel in heaven is a feeling of happiness. Even if you multiply happiness by a million, it cannot be compared to the feeling of happiness there.**

As I laid on the grass all my five senses began to operate. This was a world different from a place that had a sun. It was full of light. I was lying on the green grass and watching the flowers. I was watching the colors too many to count. My nose was smelling the fragrance there and my ears were listening to the songs there. I was listening to the songs of flowers. Everywhere was filled with songs of praises.

I could sense the beauty of heaven through my five senses. As the Bible said, 'O, taste and see that the Lord is good' (Psalm

34:8), I could taste everything there. Lying there, I felt amazing and beautiful things beyond expression. **I did not want to leave heaven.** At that time the Lord said I must leave heaven and go back. **I did not want to leave there.** "You must leave now but you never have to leave heaven," the Lord told me.

Heaven was a special place. Your appearance in heaven is like a light. So when you touch another light, the light gives off light to each other. Yet they don't harm each other because you are the light. In heaven you can hold another light, and that light is another saint.

The Lord sent me back to earth. He said, **"It is not time for you to come to heaven."** And He said, **"Go back to earth and tell my people what heaven is. Especially tell the children what you saw in heaven. When a little child begins to understand your words, tell them what you have seen."** The Lord's words shook me awake.[20]

HELL EXPERIENCED THROUGH 5 SENSES

Afterwards, the Lord said, **"Come with me."** and so I left that place. This time I did not go up; I went down. Then I pleaded

---

[20] Jones, *You Are My Friend*, 67-70.

with the Lord, "Lord, please don't take me there. O Lord, don't take me down anymore."

The place the Lord took me then was a place full of horror indescribable, and all my five senses were operating there.

There I could also hear with my ears, and I heard wretched screams without an end. These sounds made my ears miserable. They were like the sound of a chalk against a chalkboard, or the sound of a nail screeching against a metal. These sounds were heard continuously. And I cried out to the Lord, "Lord, please shut my ears." But the Lord said that was not possible. "These sounds will be heard by people in hell for eternity," said the Lord. All the sounds I heard in hell were a thousand times worse and evil than any horrible sound people can hear on earth.

The next level was my eyes being opened. I was at a loss as to what to do. Everything I saw made me miserable and depressed. There was no beauty found there. There was no light but darkness. There were only suffering, anguish, and pain. There were continuous sounds of people screaming and crying. Such horror continued on for eternity. In hell there was absolutely no comfort or hope. What I saw with my eyes was continual anxiety and sadness and grief. Everything I saw and heard was full of horror.

Then I began to smell. The smell of hell was like a decaying body. It was a smell of death. Dead, but never able to die. The horrible odor that I smelled was something I had never smelled in my life, toxic and nauseating. Some people say they smell sulfur in hell. Of course there is the smell of sulfur in hell, a horrible smell like the smell of a rotten egg. There was nothing there that smelled good.

Next I was given an opportunity to take a fruit there. Every time I tasted the fruit, it was as though my mouth was burning. Every time I tried to drink water, it tasted like fire. It felt like my inside was burning. There was a bottle of liquor and I was told to taste it. The taste of liquor in hell tasted like a hydrochloric acid, and my body felt like it was burning. My mouth and body felt like they were burning away. It felt as though hydrochloric acid had swallowed me whole. I felt this suffering would never end. It burned and swallowed me continuously. I began to cry out like numerous people in hell.

There is no more opportunity for people in hell. Their opportunity has ended. Everyone in hell had the opportunity to go to heaven while they were living on earth. They were given an opportunity to receive Jesus. But they scorned these words of opportunity and insulted and persecuted the people giving the message of Jesus. In hell they finally realized clearly what they had rejected.

Fifth, what happened to me in hell was that I was able to feel emotions. The feelings I felt there was something I could not explain, full of oppression and depression. It felt as though I was about to go insane. It felt like I was falling down, and no matter how much I fell, it was never ending. It was a complete darkness, without an end. There if you were trying to touch something, something like a scorpion or an insect was biting you.

There were numerous snakes there. They continually bit you. They were poisonous snakes. I could feel poison spreading throughout my body. However, in hell it was impossible to die. Hell was a place where people could not die for eternity.

I asked the Lord, **"Is there an end in hell?"** The Lord said, **"There is no end in hell. This is an eternal punishment."** The Lord said, **"I already had warned them but they chose to reject me and choose hell."**

The Lord told me, **"Come with me."** Then I was moved to another level. There I went to a man whom I had met in real life several weeks ago before I had this experience. The man's wife was a good Christian. I went to him to share the gospel. But the man scorned me and the gospel.

He said, "I will have a party. I will have fun with another

woman. When I come back finally, my wife will give up being a foolish Christian and will wait for me, and from then on she will always obey my words." He had five children then. At that time I was coming back after leaving his house with a complete feeling of failure. The Lord said to me then, "That was the last opportunity given to him!"

He was at a golden time of his life. He was a cement construction worker and was strong and healthy. He was full of selfishness and self-centeredness. A month after I shared the gospel with him, he died of pneumonia. When I was in hell, I saw him there.

The place was full of dark smoke, and it was difficult to see what was in front. The pot hanging from the ceiling swung left and right like a pendulum. He screamed,

"Ah, I didn't know there was a real place called hell. I scorned the man who told me about hell. Ah, there is a real hell! I used to go to church and they told me I was fine, and so I thought I was fine, but they lied to me! When I went to the hospital, the doctor told me I was very healthy and I just had a cold and people said it's just a minor ailment! But I died of cold and now I'm in hell!"

He kept repeating the words full of regret and agony over and over again. He kept repeating these words continually in

his time of eternity in hell. When I looked inside the pot, there was no body, just his head.

I asked the Lord, "Lord, where are the demons here?" The place was a completely lonely place, where he could not even converse with demons, where no one listened to his regretful gibberish talk. He just kept repeating these words of regret over and over again. Hell was a place where bad memories can never be erased. While he was living on earth, numerous people shared of Jesus and gave him opportunity, but he was tormented by those regretful and painful moments when he rejected the gospel.

> "Then they will go forth and look on the corpses of the men who have transgressed against Me. For their worm will not die and their fire will not be quenched; and they will be an abhorrence to all mankind." (Isaiah 66:24, NASB)

Isaiah 66 says the worms in hell will never die. The worm is a memory of a person. He will remember everything that he did on earth. He will remember every bad thing he did.

But in heaven there is no such memory. In heaven there is no memory of bad things you did on earth. When you go to heaven every bad memory is completely erased from your mind.

But hell is different. The worms in hell will never die and will bring misery to that person. Bad memories will be continually remembered by the people in hell. The pain will never end.

The experience of hell through my five senses brought me pain. I was so miserable I screamed. Then the Lord took me out of hell and said,

"**Warn all the people on earth. It is not my will for them to go to hell. It is their will. I gave them a free will to choose where they will spend eternity. People who go to heaven will be with me and the people who go to hell will spend eternity with their idols and demons that they have sought after. Go back to earth and warn them of this. Tell them that hell is far bigger and more evil and harder to endure than anything they can think or imagine. Warn them that hell is real. Go back to the world and share the message of salvation. That is my will. Everyone who chooses me out of their free will is going to receive salvation.**"[21]

---

21 Ibid., 70-74

7

Elder Young-moon Park

The following famous testimony is the experience of Elder Young-moon Park from before he was a believer.

MY WAYWARD LIVING IN THE DARKNESS

I was born in a small town in Jeollanam-do, Korea and lived in the city of Gwangju until 1979. I was short in height and puny in size, but I was living a very messy life as a prodigal son.

I lived in the same depraved way until 1984, but I did not have any criminal record until then. My family was there to help, but money and loyalty of friends in that world also got me away from being convicted. Eventually I was involved in an accident that led to an accidental homicide and was locked away at Yeongdeungpo Detention Center for 100 days. Waiting for visitors became a daily routine while I was locked up.

The Betrayal of My Wife

However, my wife who lived with me didn't come for a visitation even once throughout those 100 days. When I finished 100 days of incarceration, I came out of the detention center with a heart full of hate. I found out that our children were already sent to a relative in a rural area and my wife was gone without a trace. I searched for her frantically and finally met her at her parents' house in the summer of 1985 for the first time in several months. And her first word to me was, 'Divorce me.'

Feeling betrayed, I immediately lunged towards my wife to kill her with a paring knife that I was using to peel a fruit. Then, she quickly ran away. I closed my eyes and looked back on my life while holding that knife in my hand.

'Do I need to continue to live?'

At that time, I didn't have any will to live in this world. Without any more thought, I tried to kill myself using the knife that I was holding. Right at the moment of stabbing my stomach, my father-in-law urgently tripped my foot and knocked me down. But as I fell down, the knife went about 7 cm into my calf. After an emergency treatment at the hospital, the doctor urged me to have surgery within 1 hour. Without the surgery, I would lose the leg. He said that the blood vessels that were needed for flexing the leg were all cut up, so without the surgery, my leg would start to rot.

Hearing this, I thought, 'Why should I get the surgery done? I was going to die anyway.'

Even though I didn't have any faith at the time, I wailed and screamed, "I will give my eyes to the blind, my heart to a person suffering from a heart disease, my kidneys to a person without kidney, and give away all the organs to people who need them. Please kill me without any pain!" When I woke up and opened my eyes, it was 13 hours later. I felt pain in my leg and saw that there was a white bandage wrapped around my leg. The relief of not having an amputation on my leg quickly passed. I called for doctors and nurses, threw anything that I could grab and cursed with unspeakable foul language. I screamed, "Why did you save my life? Why did you keep me alive in vain?"

The Plan to Murder My Wife's Family

After being discharged, I couldn't suppress the rage that came up every time I looked at the scar on my right leg that looked like a cut on a fish belly. As an old Korean saying goes, 'You despise your mother-in-law who tries to stop her son even more than your abusive husband,' I now hated my annoying in-laws much more than my wife who betrayed me. I despised them to death.

So, I made up my mind to kill all eight of them at once, including little children, in one place by any means. Then, just like a criminal who surveys the site for his crime, I went to their 2-story house on the mountain and observed them several times.

I thought because there was no night curfew, I could block all the exits of the house, prepare gasoline and set it on fire in the late night while everyone was asleep. That way I could kill everyone in the house before the firefighters reach the house on the top of a mountain. With that thought in my mind, I went to my hometown Gwangju first.

I decided to drink poison mixed into my favorite drink and leave this world as well, when I could confirm that all of them died. However, when I thought that this would be my final moment, a face popped up in my head. It was the face of my mother who gave birth to me. While I was incarcerated in Yeongdeungpo Detention Center for 100 days, she visited me repeatedly from Gwangju to Seoul, which is about 3 hours away, in the cold winter. I wanted to see my mother's face once more before my last day in this world. So I went to my hometown, Gwangju.

9:50 p.m., April 3, 1986

On April 3, 1986, I bumped into a friend from Seoul on the street while I was in Gwangju. We both loved to drink, so we started to drink early in the afternoon at a pub. While we filled each other's cup and drank, he told me some gossip from his neighborhood. He heard that my estranged wife was working at a pub in Seoul as a bottle girl. At that moment I was caught in a blaze of anger. I wanted to go right away, so I asked him, "When are you going back to Seoul?" He answered, "I'll be on the train to Seoul at 10:40 p.m. tonight." I said, "Good. You can go ahead of me to the train station and buy 2 tickets. We'll meet around 10:30 p.m. at the station.'" Then I came back home, set an alarm for 9:50 p.m., and slept. After waking up from sleep, I used the bathroom, then laid down on my tummy and smoked a cigarette. I was deeply meditating on the plan to kill my in-law's. 'If I start off tonight, I'll be arriving early tomorrow morning, so I can proceed with my plan anytime between two days, tomorrow evening or early morning the next day. I'll confirm with my own eyes after completely killing off everyone in that family with any means possible.'

That was the moment, only 40 minutes before getting on the train to Seoul. From outside, there was a booming voice repeatedly speaking twice. It was a very loud and strong voice that could burst one's ear drums.

HEAVEN

The voice said, **"You there! Look here!"** (This was before accepting Jesus as my Lord and Savior, so I think that is why the voice said "You there! Look here!" instead of "My beloved son Young-moon!") to call me. It was a voice that I have never heard in my entire life.

That voice was not like the voice of a man, but it rather sounded like a booming sound from a big record player or echoing from the top of a mountain.

It was very strange, so I went out the door to look for the person who made that sound, but I couldn't find anyone. I came back to the room thinking that it was weird and as I was about to light a half-burned cigarette that I didn't finish, I felt the room suddenly become bright. The door on the room had hanji paper pasted on it, and seven colors of the rainbow that one can often see after the rain falls across on that door. (And he who sat there had the appearance of jasper and carnelian, and around the throne was a rainbow that had the appearance of an emerald. -Rev. 4:3)

The Angels and the Golden Carriage

Then I saw something coming down from above in the middle of that light and when I looked closely, it was **a man clothed in white**. The figure looked human like us. **Although I couldn't find the eyes, nose, and mouth on his face because they weren't clearly visible, his head looked like a red flame that was as big as a full moon. And he was shining light on my face, blinding my eyes.** (his face was like the sun shining in full strength. -Rev. 1:16, his face like the appearance of lightning -Dan. 10:6, For God … has shone in our hearts to give the light of the knowledge of the glory of God in the face of Jesus Christ -2 Cor. 4:6) As soon as the figure that had a shape of a man clothed in white came down and stayed, a square carriage followed down right after.

There were three seats on that carriage. The middle seat was empty and the two seats on either side were occupied by two people dressed in white. I was able to make out eyes, nose, and mouth on them, and I couldn't express in words how beautiful they were. The color of the carriage was brilliant gold, not like the usual yellowish gold color seen in a gold necklace or gold ring.

The gold rings and gold necklaces that people wear look

yellow and they are recognized as gold because people say they are gold, but you do not see them shine brightly. This carriage, on the other hand, was shining intensely with brilliance. Also, the white clothes that two people on either side had on were covered densely with pea-sized jewels that looked like pearls or diamonds and they gave off blindingly sparkling light as well.

If someone who believed in Jesus saw this scene, he would have been overjoyed, calling God or Jesus… But I despised religious fanatics the most and I could not think of it in that way.

My Spirit Came out of My Body

I kept my red jacket on after going to the bathroom, and when I looked at the door again, I saw a person who wore the same clothes about to sit in that empty middle seat of the golden carriage and turn his face toward me. Then, I realized that the person was actually me.

I exclaimed, "Oh!" and touched my body to check. I was clearly sitting in the room and another me was sitting in the golden carriage also, as if I was looking at my reflection in a mirror… (I know a man in Christ who fourteen years ago was caught up to the third heaven—whether in the body or out of the body I do not know, God knows. -2 Cor. 12:2)

The Golden Road of Heaven

As soon as I sat down in the carriage, it started off. The human-shaped light led the way and the carriage followed behind. Then, I heard music resounding softly. It was not like worldly music, nor traditional music or pop songs. **I was listening intently to the sound of music that I was hearing for the first time and when I looked forward, I was very surprised. The road was not bent but completely straight and was not made with asphalt or dirt. It was shining with a golden color, the same color as the carriage. It stretched as far as I could see and looked as if the road was paved by pouring gold all over it, or had gold-plating done to it. Anyways, it was glowing with a splended radiant golden hue.** (the street of the city was pure gold, like transparent glass -Rev. 21:21)

The Flower Garden in Heaven

The human-shaped light glided on that golden road floating a few inches from the ground and the carriage that I was on was also floating a few inches from the surface as it followed the light. When I looked at each side of the road while sitting on the carriage, there were flower gardens which stretched as far as I could see without any obstruction. And in those flower gardens, there were many different colors and types of flowers that were impossible to count. Innumerable birds and butterflies were flying on top of those countless flowers as well. I also heard the sound of birds that I had seen for the first time, and it could not be described as bird sounds, but it was more like joyous laughing of birds that was clear and lively. When I close my eyes, I can see that beautiful scene of that moment, but it is impossible to describe. The countless flowers were not wilted but looked alive and moving. And these flowers looked as if they were smiling sweetly as well.

The Fragrance of Heaven

Furthermore, I had never smelled such a beautiful fragrance in this world before. My sense of smell was on the dull side usually. So, when I went hiking with my friends and saw flowers, my friends would feel intoxicated with the flower scent, but I could not smell any good scent even when they cut the flower and put it under my nose. But the scent that came from the flower garden permeated even into my nose as I sat on the carriage and I was almost intoxicated by it. It's very regrettable not being able to describe in words, verbal as well as written, the floral scent that is delicately sweet, something that I have never experienced in this world. It felt like several days passed while floating in that beautiful and fragrant flower garden listening to the mysterious sound of music.

The Dancing Angels

Then on the lawn, I saw some people who wore the same white clothes as the two on either side of me. They were floating on the lawn inside the flower bed and dancing as if flying to the soft sound of music. I didn't know at that time, but I was told later on that those people who were dancing on the lawn and the two people beside me were all angels. I was actually looking at angels whom I only heard of, but I didn't realize it at the moment.

There were countless angels hovering and dancing to the far end, as far as I could see. How beautiful the brides are when they adorn their white dresses on their wedding day! But the shining faces of the angels wearing white clothes with big and bright smiles like a peony flower could not be compared to the faces of people in this world.

Seeing My Uncle in Heaven

After the area where the angels were dancing, I passed through a place that looked the same as the previous area and there were people in it. There were not only Asians like us Koreans there, but an assembly of people from all over the world such as Black people, White people, people with dark hair, white hair, and yellow hair. When the human-shaped light shone its light on the area where countless people stayed, I saw the face of my uncle, my mother's brother, who died of an illness.

When he was alive, he lived close by for a period of time in the neighborhood where I lived. **He lived in walking distance about 10 minutes away from my place, but I didn't visit my mother's family from early on because he was considered a Jesus freak.** However, when he became critically ill, relatives from as far as Gwangju where he was originally from visited him. Until then, I did not visit him once, but regardless of his religion, I thought it was too disrespectful not to see him before he died. So, I made up my mind to see his face one last time. That was one week before he died. It was in the middle of summer and quite hot, so he was wearing a sleeveless undershirt and shorts, and I couldn't believe his wretched appearance to be of a human appearance. He looked on with his sunken eyes and cheeks, and I couldn't figure out whether he was breathing or not.

Honestly, he did not look alive with his stomach and back stuck together and his bony ribs showing through the undershirt. Even with my dull sense of smell, it smelt like something rotting and I couldn't bear that odor, so I came outside to smoke a cigarette. My aunt was washing rice under the outside water tap, because it was lunchtime then. I was looking at the face of my aunt who was washing rice for a while and thought that she was really pathetic. For some reason, she didn't show any anxieties or worries on her face, even though her husband was on the brink of dying, possibly tonight or tomorrow morning or even right now. Also the fact that she looked fat as if she ate alone indifferent to her husband's condition and even at that moment, the scene of her making lunch made me furious. So I blasted her.

"Auntie! Why can't he get better and is lying miserably there if God or Jesus, whatever you believe in, is real? You even sold the house…"

They had sold the house which was really nice and moved to a small hut to pay for his hospital bills. It was unbelievable that all five of them were living in such a small hut. If they believed in Jesus, they should have lived better, but they became extremely poor and on top of that, he was on the brink of death due to his illness. It was so pathetic. However, my abrupt protest didn't even upset her. Instead, she smiled and said, "Because he is going to a much better world than this world."

I was once more dumbfounded by her answer.

"When a person dies, he rots in dirt. What do you mean by this world and the other world?"

You live and die in this world once and that is it. How can there be a better world or a terrible world? I thought that was a made-up story by gossipers and felt frustrated and repulsed. So, I came home without eating lunch with them.

However, when I saw my uncle in that place, his appearance was not the same as what I saw before he died: skinny with bones protruding, unable to distinguish whether he is alive or dead. He had the face and build of his younger self, the one that I saw when I was in my 3rd or 4th grade. When I was young and lived in a rural area, he would bring fancy new shoes which I had never seen in my life and made me very happy. He had that fresh appearance of his 30's.

The clothing he was wearing was something that I had never seen in this world. He wore a robe that had the same color as the carriage, a bright golden color, which was intensely brilliant.

There were countless people under the light and they were all smiling broadly just like my uncle. They looked very peaceful and free; I could not see any anxieties or worries of the world in them.

I thought it would be over once a person dies. However, I saw clearly with my own eyes that there is a better world afterwards when the light shone on none other than my own uncle. I was not dreaming. I did not see him while in a trance during a prayer. 40 minutes before going to Seoul to kill off eight lives, I was pulled by the light that was as big as a full moon clad in white clothes, and then I saw my uncle in the Kingdom of God.

The Golden House Prepared in Heaven

As the carriage continued on the road, we passed an area that brilliant golden houses were built on. I asked the angels sitting beside me, "Where are you taking me? And where is this place?", but no answer came from them. But when we reached the area with brilliant golden houses, the angel who sat on my right said in a clear voice, **"This is heaven."** The houses stretched as far as I could see and they were innumerable.

The carriage that I was on moved slowly like a slow moving car, so I couldn't see the inside of the house closely. The Only things that I could see were the roof and doorposts of those houses in the same brilliant golden color as the carriage. It's regrettable not being able to describe how it is built with words. If I could draw the house, I would, but it looked impossible to put it onto a canvas; it was built with gold and jewels in splendor and it was shining ever so brightly. Meanwhile, I was thinking that if I could bring one of these houses down on the earth, I would be the richest person in the world.

Occasionally I would see a newly-built house that was waiting for its owner, all clean and decorated neatly in this world. All the houses that I saw there looked like they were all built recently and decorated neatly. They looked as though they were waiting for their owners, all ready to move in immediately.

HELL

Then suddenly, the carriage went into the darkness. (And cast the worthless servant into the outer darkness. In that place there will be weeping and gnashing of teeth. -Matt. 25:30) From the fragrant flower bed to the place where the splendid house was, I would look back for some time as I missed seeing them. But here, the front and back both were pitch black and I could only see the human-shaped light leading the carriage, and the immediate surrounding of the carriage. I got scared all of a sudden. I thought they were going to kill me after showing me all those beautiful things that were not of this world. I felt frightened as we continued on.

Seeing My Father in Hell

At that moment, the human-shaped light shone down in the darkness and when I looked closely, I saw the face of my father who had died 6 years ago.

"What! What is going on?"

Again, I was shocked. **When my father was alive, he was a Confucian scholar who worked at a Confucian school for a very long time. He became one of the executives in the school, which might be translated to an elder in the church. He was in an important position at the school, and hearing just the first syllable of the name "Jesus" would drive him mad.**

I was able to see my father again in that darkness by the human-shaped light that was as big as a full moon. He looked the same as when he was on his deathbed 6 years ago, swollen all over due to his illness. Many blue vipers with triangular heads covered his feet up to his ankles. These vipers slithered all over my father's body biting, tearing, and scratching, so that all of his body was covered in blood. I closed and opened my eyes several times, but it was really my father.

Standing there I cried and called out, "Father, father!" several times, but it seemed that he couldn't hear my desperate cries at all. He held onto his swollen tummy, tried to escape from the countless vipers here and there, and suffered. It was a dreadful scene that I could not bear to see. Under the light, there were so many people like my father who were suffering from the countless vipers that were flicking their tongues. I thought that once a person lives a life in the world, dies, and rots in the dirt, that would be the end of it. But it was not so. I met other people there and was able to see my father who died 6 years ago. The appearance of my father ripped my heart to pieces. It was unbearable to see.

I cried as I watched my suffering father, and screamed "Father!" When I looked on, the light spotlighted another area. It was like using a flashlight to walk in the countryside at night time. The light only illuminates a small area at a time, so as you move your flashlight to shine on one area, the previously visible area becomes dark and cannot be seen again. When the light moved, the area where my father was became completely dark and I was not able to see him again.

The next scene was so terrible; it was unbearable to see with human eyes.

Seeing My Uncle in Hell

There were many people flocking around in this area. I wondered why and looked closely. I saw something like a round brazier with a width that could not be measured. It was very wide. On top of it, there was an iron plate that looked similar to a grill. It had holes shaped like a net. Innumerable people flocked here and there on that iron plate. There was red fire burning underneath the iron plate that looked like a grill, and in the middle, there was blue flame following people around. **They were frantically trying to avoid that flame by flocking here and there in complete chaos.** (And if your hand or your foot causes you to sin, cut it off and throw it away. It is better for you to enter life crippled or lame than with two hands or two feet to be thrown into the eternal fire. And if your eye causes you to sin, tear it out and throw it away. It is better for you to enter life with one eye than with two eyes to be thrown into the hell of fire. -Matt. 18:8-9, where their worm does not die and the fire is not quenched. For everyone will be salted with fire. -Mark 9:48-49)

In the place where the human-shaped light illuminated, I saw the face of my uncle, my father's elder brother, among many people. They were in excruciating pain because of the extreme temperatures in that burning fire. I was astonished and called out "Uncle! Uncle!" to him who was suffering and scorching in the fire amongst many people. It seemed like he couldn't hear me; his only focus was on avoiding the flame just like other people there. The flame did not seem to burn the flesh, so no one was blackened or reddened on their skin.

I think it continuously burns without being extinguished and scalding the flesh. Many people flocked around trying to avoid the scorching fire and also to avoid falling into the hole. While I cried, the light illuminated another place and the area that my uncle was in became pitch black again, so I couldn't see anymore.

Seeing My Friend in Hell

At the third place where the light illuminated, I saw my friend who died in a motorcycle accident in 1984. It had been 2 years since he died when I saw him there. Three black serpents were wrapped around him. And these were so tightly wrapped that his face had turned blue. I was not able to see what he was wearing because the serpents were completely surrounding his entire body. Two serpents were on his right and left and one serpent was behind his head, flicking their tongues. The serpents were huge; a size that could not be seen in this world. It was so gross and terrible to watch. I called out his name several times, but he didn't respond to my voice. He continued to suffer miserably within the tight coil of black serpents. Then, the light moved slowly and the area became dark again, so I could not see him anymore.

Seeing One of My In-laws and a Person from My Hometown

At the fourth place that the light illuminated, I saw people stuck in a slough, deep swamp, up to their waist. There, I saw a small black animal that looked like a newborn piglet with a pointy mouth and sharp teeth. It was hitting, tearing and scratching people from the front, back and sides and making them bloody. They could not run away from it and were moving only to the right and left to avoid it. Among these countless suffering people, I saw the faces of two people who I used to know, my in-law and a person from my hometown. People couldn't move because they were stuck in the slough, but strangely, not even one of those animals were bogged down as they swarmed around. Those numerous animals crawled eerily on the slough and were biting, scratching and torturing people who could not move.

These four places that I saw so far were unthinkably horrible. I thought I might be dreaming. Yet, I saw clearly with my own eyes desperately miserable sights of my father, uncle, friend and in-law in the darkness that was impossible to distinguish from front to back.

When I shared my testimony of seeing my in-law suffering in the darkness later on, a person who wasn't a church-goer asked me this question. **"They say that anyone can go to heaven**

if he attends church. Why was your in-law who went to church for about a year in that place?" (Not everyone who says to me, 'Lord, Lord,' will enter the kingdom of heaven, but the one who does the will of my Father who is in heaven. -Matt. 7:21)

At that time, I didn't know whether my in-law attended church or not, so I couldn't answer that question. Later on, because it was strange to me as well, I asked my brother who is a pastor.

"Why is my in-law who went to church suffering terribly in that slough?"

My brother said that one cannot be saved without accepting Jesus as his Lord and Saviour in his heart. Even if he attended church for a year, or for 10 years, he cannot be saved. On the other hand, if one believes that there is heaven and hell after death, and accepts Jesus as his Lord and Savior in his heart, he would be given salvation. Even if one attends church for just one day, he would be saved.

After a while, I asked a close friend of the in-law whom I saw in hell about him. He said, "He was sick and he heard from somewhere that he would be healed if he went to church, so I think he was merely going back and forth on the threshold of a church."

THE JUDGMENT SEAT

When the carriage stopped for the first time, I was in a place called **'The Judgment Seat'.** (And the sea gave up the dead who were in it, Death and Hades gave up the dead who were in them, and they were judged, each one of them, according to what they had done. -Rev. 20:13)

There was a book called 'Memoir' which recorded all the sins that I committed through my eyes, mouth, hands, feet, and mind, since I was born. It had a record of dates from the first day that I sinned until last April 3rd, and it was marked with several letters and colors that I could not recognize.

General Sins

Sins that I committed were shown to me one by one from that memoir. I had committed 132 kinds of sins while in this world. They were organized as such; in the category of 'Thievery', when and what was stolen were written in detail with the date and specifics of the act, and there were so many of them. And in one category of 'Lies', there were so many entries as well. **Among them, there were most entries under the mistakes that I made when I was drunk. I loved to drink, so I think that is the reason why I had that many slip-ups.**

The book thus categorized and organized those 132 kinds

of sins that I committed through my eyes, mouth, hands, and feet. However, there was one category that was written in big red words without any more entries underneath. I asked what this was and the answer was 'Murder'. I looked closely, surprised by it. It was the motorcycle accident that killed my friend in 1984. Even though I didn't kill him intentionally, it was written as murder because he died on my account. Come to think of it now, I understand how precious one person's life is. Especially when I think of my friend who is suffering in hell wrapped around by serpents, I feel that a person's life is tremendously precious.

Special Sins

Additionally, I found out about two sins that were not considered as a sin in democratic countries such as South Korea, but were considered as sin there. The first is not believing in Jesus and the second is persecuting believers. In my memoir, it listed these two sins as categories and there were numerous entries under each category. **My sins of the past included obviously not attending church, tearing and burning the Bible and hymn book, swearing, loathing and even kicking and slapping an evangelizing Christian. These were recorded accurately including dates and times.**

And it even had a detailed record of the time when I stole a ten-dollar bill from my mother's closet. I was in my 4th grade, and bought and ate cookies with my friends with that money. It was astounding to find recordings of things that happened many years ago but had been forgotten. Under 132 categories of sins, the book recorded countless sins completely in detail. Of those sins, there were some of which I didn't even remember.

In that place, I asked a question that was in my mind.

"Why me? Why wasn't this place shown to someone like my brother who loves Jesus so much and is dedicated to His work wholeheartedly? Why was this place shown to me, a sinner, who loathes Jesus and has done every one of the things that the world calls sin?"

The angel standing beside me answered.

"Someone like your brother doesn't need to be here. The reason is when a person like you sees heaven and hell with his own eyes, he can believe and testify to other people."

This is right. I was able to believe Jesus only after seeing it personally and testify as thus, but I pray that you believe without seeing it as the Bible states, "Blessed are those who have not seen and yet have believed." (John 20:29) and are greatly blessed.

WILL YOU BELIEVE?

The carriage started again. And then all of a sudden, I heard in a loud and strong voice saying, **"Will you believe?"** (For God so loved the world, that he gave his only Son, that whoever believes in him should not perish but have eternal life. -John 3:16) That voice was the same voice that said "You there! Look here!" which I heard in a room 40 minutes before leaving for Seoul to murder the whole family. I lifted my head to see where that voice was coming from. Then, I knew instantly that the voice was coming from the human-shaped light which was as big as a full moon and led the carriage that I was on. And the voice seemed to ask if I firmly believed in everything that was shown to me until now.

Throughout my life, I had never called upon Father God even once and didn't know the meaning of the word, 'Lord'. But at that moment, I was unconsciously kneeling on the carriage and had accepted Him by saying, **"Lord, I believe."**

After that, the human-shaped light said, **"When you go back to the world, testify to the people that there is heaven and hell exactly as you have seen without adding or subtracting from it."**

The mission of a mailman is completed when the letter is

delivered to the address that is written on the envelope. It is not required of him to read the content of the letter to the receiver. In the same way, my mission is done when I testify about heaven and hell as I have seen without adding or taking anything away. I was not given a mission of planting faith in you who are reading this testimony. Whether you believe it or not, that's up to you. I pray that none of you who read this testimony goes to that frightful hell that I saw.[22]

---

[22] Beloved Church TV. (2022, April 3). *The Testimony of Heaven and Hell by Elder Park Young-moon* (in Korean) [Video]. YouTube. https://youtu.be/nB5BGBS2pH4

8

Pastor Ivan Tuttle

The following testimony is from an excerpt of the book, *A Journey to Hell, Heaven, and Back* by Pastor Ivan Tuttle. Pastor Tuttle visited our church as a guest speaker in the past. The other testimonies in this book are from those who have already passed away and Pastor Tuttle is the only one who is still living. Thus, we asked for his permission and he gladly allowed us to cite his book here. I deeply thank Pastor Ivan Tuttle for this.

This book was written about the death, or what society calls an NDE (Near Death Experience), I had back in 1978. At that time in my life, I was not living a very good life; at 26 years old I was mixed up in drugs and my life was spiraling out of control. I made some bad choices for my life back then, but little did I know that my mother would be so instrumental in helping me back.

I went straight to hell when I died. It was a horrible place with people screaming and yelling constantly and begging to get out. **Some people had been there for thousands of years, and they would beg everyone new being brought into hell, asking them to help them get out.** Hell was the most horrible place I had ever seen, and since that experience I plan on staying out.[23]

GOING TO HELL

Around 9:20 that night, I was woken up by something or someone grabbing my left wrist and holding on to it very tight, pulling me right up out of my body. I turned around to see my lifeless body just lying there. I was shocked and kept trying to break free from this horrible thing. I even tried to turn the light on in the room to no avail; my hand went right through the wall. This thing had a death grip on my wrist and I could not get free. I looked around at everything in the room just trying to think of a way to escape when all of a sudden we started to move through space and time into this horrible

---

23 Ivan Tuttle, *A Journey to Heaven and Back*, (Charlotte, NC: It's Supernatural!, 2020) 10.

darkness. We moved so fast that time didn't matter, and where it took me was the most horrific place I had ever seen, heard, or smelled.

I could hear people screaming; at first the sound was way off in the distance, but within seconds the screams were so loud it was as if they were coming from right beside me. The shrieks were beyond anything I have ever heard before, and the stench was indescribably repulsive. The sense of hopelessness I felt in this place was totally overwhelming. The realization finally hit me that I was in **hell. No, this was not a dream, and it was not a drug-induced hallucination. I was dead and I was in hell.** All hope and expectation of life was gone. The evil spirit that had hold of me had begun laughing at me. It was incredibly grotesque looking and had the strength of a hundred men. **As I heard the screams and shrieks of the people there, I could feel their pain in a way considerably beyond what we typically feel here on earth. Our earthly minds and bodies cannot begin to understand or exist with that type of pain. The heat there became unbearable,** although I didn't ever see actual flames. **Why was I in hell and, I thought, what did I do to deserve this? I was a pretty good kid and I even went to Bible college for a little while. I didn't hurt anyone or kill anybody, so why was I in hell?** Then I realized that the answers didn't really matter because I knew there was no escape and I was trapped there forever—and I do mean forever.

At first I didn't realize that I was still moving down toward the center of hell. I wasn't quite there yet; I had only been on the outskirts of hell. All the while, the demon continued to laugh at me with the most hideous sound my ears had ever heard. It was even worse than the deep, echoing demon voices in the movies. As this demon took me deeper into hell, the smell got so terrible that it permeated my whole being, and the sounds of people screaming literally pierced my being. However, I still tried fighting this evil spirit that had me, and I was screaming like the rest of the people there. I could still feel that insufferable heat coming up from below me, too.

Though words seem utterly inadequate in trying to explain this experience, I will try my best to convey to you the hopelessness and horrifying feelings one has when they're in hell. People were all around me. I bumped into some, and they were screaming as loud as they could and cursing God and **yelling at me to please tell their children or other loved ones that hell is for real.** They knew it was useless, yet they still screamed and cried out in pain. **The pain and anguish there is beyond any suffering you have ever known; it literally engulfs your whole being. Kind of like the worst toothache or headache you have**

ever had times a thousand and it is throughout your whole being.

Imagine falling from an airplane at 35,000 feet up and you have no parachute and nothing but concrete below to land on. You know you are going to die. **Well, that hopeless feeling you have going all the way down to certain death—that is what hell is like times ten thousand.** There is so much more I could tell you about hell, more ways to try and describe the despair, agony, and suffering, but what it all comes down to is this—just understand, once you are in hell, it is too late to ask God into your life. It's too late to change your ways or to send a message to others about how awful hell really is.

This heinous thing that had ahold of me was taking me further down, and as I felt the heat getting hotter I began to scream as loud as I could. I cried out to God but felt it didn't matter. I thought He wouldn't answer my prayers now that I was dead; I'd had that choice while I was alive. Nothing I could do had any meaning now; I was nothing and felt nothing but complete hopelessness. It was dark and frightening. People were still yelling at me as I passed by them. They screamed, "Get me out of here, please!" Most seemed to be locked in place by something unseen; it was too dark for me to tell, but as I moved past them I could see that they could not move.

They just grabbed me and tried desperately to hold on to me.

In this state of being, you don't have a body of the type you had when you were alive in your earthly body, but you do have a body. You feel pain, and you see and hear everything with perfect vision and hearing. But the pain in hell is unbelievably worse than anything on earth. At least with earthly pain when it gets too bad you can pass out and escape from it, but not in hell. If you get a cut in the flesh, it only hurts where you got cut, but in hell if you cut your finger it hurts throughout your whole being.

I'm sure I have not adequately described the creatures in hell—what they looked like, smelled like, and what they did. There were some creatures that were very big, about ten or twelve feet tall and they were very grotesque with rotted flesh and a smell that matched. Many of them had long, disfigured arms and legs and they were so strong that they could rip you in half. **There were others that seemed to just slither around like huge snakes. I could see many of them going to the center of hell and heading back to earth. I assumed they were being instructed on what to do by satan himself and they were returning to earth to do it. Some of these beasts were creatures of deception; they would go and enter a body in order to possess it. Usually that would be a very pretty woman or handsome man** who then would entice someone to have sex with them. These same demonic spirits would also get people to believe in things like fortune telling, horoscopes, mind reading, etc. These evil spirits would actually work in people with these gifts, though in actuality they were really just well-planned guesses as they have had thousands of years to learn all about people. The twists and turns these demon spirits would do to people and the lies they led them to believe were purposefully deceptive.

People do not realize that many things on earth have demonic beginnings—like stories about vampires, werewolves, white magic, witches, trolls, and ogres. Even the movies where there are supposed to be good witches and warlocks that fight evil come from a demonic background as well. You should also know that video games that have extreme violence, murder, extra lives when you battle evil forces, and the like all have a demonic presence in them. I don't understand why people are so blind to this today, but that, too, is a trick of the devil.

Parents, wake up! This happened to me back in 1978 and I was able to see these types of games before they were ever even invented or released. There is no time after you die; it is forever and you are leading your children straight to hell by letting them play these games! Just look back at kids from the '60s and '70s and then look at the kids in the '80s and '90s and

you can see the difference. Now look at the kids today—there is very little communication with them, they are always playing these games and ignoring their parents. You go to church and your children do, too, and they seem like good kids, but there is a deep, dark side you do not know about your own children when you allow them access to these things. I understand your kids keep telling you that everyone else does it and so and so allows their kids to do it, but that still doesn't make it alright. Even if the pastor's kids at your church are allowed to play those games or watch those movies it's still opening up a doorway for demonic powers to enter your home and your children.

There are millions of types of demons of numerous sizes, shapes, and assignments, but they all have the same overall mission and that is to destroy your relationship with God any possible way they can. They can come to you in the form of just about anything here on earth, but make no mistake about it, they are here. **In hell there was talk about how the demons were going to rob, steal, and destroy parents' relationships with their children. They plan to do it with books, videos, games, music, teachers, and even at times our own government will help.** Demons can do things we as humans can't do, so surround your children with prayer on a daily basis. Some of you might think this is strange, but it is so important to pray over

your children and plead the blood of Jesus over them, because nothing the devil has ever come up with can penetrate the blood of Jesus!

Think of it like this—back when the Israelites were in Egypt and the death angel was sent to kill all of the first born, if you had lamb's blood on your door posts the angel of death could not harm you. Jesus is the Lamb of God and His blood was shed for all of us and by speaking the name of Jesus, pleading the blood of Jesus over your children, you keep the demonic forces from your children. But that is not all you need to do. **You need to get rid of those books, CDs, videos and games, etc., or you are inviting the demons back in your house. As parents, you must do your best to keep your children away from those types of entertainment.** These things I have seen with my own eyes and have experienced firsthand. **Hell is real, make no mistake about it, and you are going there unless you ask Jesus into your life.** Hell is not something to play with; there I was trapped for all eternity, never to escape. **I saw so many people there who never thought they would end up in hell. These were good people—some were even former pastors of churches, deacons, Sunday school teachers, some familiar men and women from our past—very good people, but they were doomed to hell forever.**

I heard more screams and more people crying out, and I knew for sure I was going into the pit of hell and that I could never return. I just wish I could get through to you what that felt like. It's kind of like that dream you have when you are just about asleep or just nodded off and all of a sudden you feel like you are falling. Well, it's like that, except you don't wake up and shake it off, you just keep falling and falling and falling. **There is no end to it or the torture you are put through —the sounds and the smell.** The smell is worse than rotted garbage and the worst sewer odor you could imagine, all combined with the smell of sulfur.

I knew then with certainty I was going to just be tortured and burn in hell forever. I believed the lie that marijuana was good for you because God put it on earth. Well, God may have put it on earth, but not for the purpose we are using it for. He also made cyanide, but if we use it wrong it will kill us. Some things kill the body and those things are bad, but what kills your spirit is even worse. I was lost, and to think I had all those chances to turn things around and change my life, but my own self-satisfaction was too important to me. I thought what a fool I had been; I was truly trapped and now would have to pay the price for all eternity.

MORE OF HELL

Here were things in hell that are hard to explain and even harder to describe. Once down there it is very dark, yet you can still see because you are not using your fleshly or earthly eyes but your spiritual ones. **While going through hell I met several people or souls down there as I was moving past them. Some were just everyday ordinary people, just like you and me, and some were mighty people at one time, including preachers.**

I met a girl named Mary who was only 18 when she died and she couldn't understand why she was in hell. She never really believed in God, heaven, or hell, but she does now. Mary said she was in college and was driving home for Christmas break from college when she got hit head-on by a drunk driver. She couldn't understand why God didn't forgive her because it was not her fault she died before she could accept Christ; it was the drunk's fault. Mary said she was alive for a few days in a hospital and she could hear her mother and father praying for her, but she could not do anything about it because she could not answer or move. Mary remembered them saying she was brain dead and that the doctors told her mother and father after three days they would take her off of life support if there were no brain waves. Mary could hear all this going on but couldn't do anything about it.

Finally, on the third day her mother and father were in her hospital room when the doctor came in and talked with her parents and everyone agreed to disconnect her. This scared Mary because she knew she wasn't dead yet and wanted to stay alive as long as possible—death scared her. Mary watched as her mother and father said goodbye to her and nodded for the nurse in the room to disconnect the life support. From what Mary was saying, I believe she was having an out-of-body experience or NDE. Mary said she couldn't get any air and felt like she was drowning, and she said everything felt stiff like she couldn't move any part of her body. Then this evil spirit came and took her to hell.

Many people screamed or yelled at me in hell. As soon as I saw these people, in less than a second I knew their stories. The way people communicated in hell was like talking without saying anything, but I heard them clear as a bell. One other person allowed to talk to me was a person from Asia, but I am not sure which country. He said his name, but I am not sure how to spell it; it seemed like it was Jung Sho He. **He was a jeweler back on earth and he had a wife, two sons, and a daughter. Jung believed there was no God, no heaven or hell,** and was shocked when he had a heart attack and died only to find out there was a hell and he was trapped there forever. He begged me to tell his wife and children if I could. At that time, I only knew I was staying there forever like him.

The sights in hell are nothing like what has ever been shown to man here on earth. It was worse than any picture or movie I have ever seen. Imagine solid, jagged rock walls with people attached by some invisible force, like being chained up, and these walls go on forever—over a million miles in every direction. It is dark, it stinks—the smell of rotten flesh and garbage mixed with sulfur smell and heat so hot that your flesh would melt off its bones—that is just a little idea of what hell is like. You get there, you don't leave!

Imagine everything I described about hell and then add the torture you go through all the time. You never get a break, not even for a minute. These evil spirits are there to torture you and they get such pleasure out of it. Hell is worse than having someone break every inch of every bone in your body, inch by inch, one bone at a time—slowly so it takes a whole month to do it. Yes, hell is worse than that. The demons are tearing you apart, but you don't come apart; you only rip and tear but you stay together. This pain is horrible.

I watched as some demons were tearing apart a young lady,

maybe 18 to 20 years of age. She was a beautiful young lady at one time, yet these demons have tortured her for over 400 years and they have never stopped. Imagine having someone tie your hands up to two different car bumpers and your feet at two different car bumpers and then your head tied up to another car bumper. All at once, all the cars start pulling you apart in all different directions, but you never come apart and you can't pass out. You just suffer the pain, over and over again forever and forever. That would be like a vacation in hell, because that's not even close to a minor pain there.

I saw something else that was interesting to me in hell—I saw demons fighting over who gets to torture someone. They seemed to do this a lot, especially over people who claimed to be Christians on earth but hid stuff about their real activities. I call them "fake Christians" because they claim to be a Christian, but their walk with God is nothing like Christ. They were only satisfied with pleasing themselves. That is one of the biggest lies satan has Christians believing—it's okay to want and desire things; it's okay to have an affair, God will forgive you; it's okay to steal, you need the clothes or food; it's okay to cheat on that test, you studied hard and others are cheating; it's okay to spend your money on whatever you like, you don't need to give to the Lord; it's okay to satisfy your-

self, everyone does—and the list goes on and on. Demons or evil spirits cannot be described in human words, but they are real—they do exist. There are demons in every part of this world.

Here is a shock for you—over one half of all people going to hell didn't believe in hell before they died. They thought everyone would go to heaven and that hell was what we lived like on earth or what we made of life here on earth. People who believe in gods like statues, rocks, idols—Buddhists, Muslims, Hindus, etc.—are all living a lie, and when they die they are going to be so shocked to find out that there really is a heaven and hell and there really is a God. God is not a rock or a statue, Buddha or Muhammad. He is God, the I AM, the only living God who always has been and always will be, none before and none after Him! You don't have to take my word for this —it's in the Bible. Or you can wait till you go to hell and then you will know what I am telling you is correct—but then it will be too late.[24]

ARRIVING IN HEAVEN

All of a sudden, I heard a voice like a mighty roar of thunder

---

[24] Tuttle, *A Journey to Heaven and Back*, 22-30.

that said, **"It is not his time yet. His mother has been praying for him since he was a little boy. You must release him now; I made a promise!"** The evil spirit that had hold of me released me immediately, and I seemed to just fly through space upward and out of hell in seconds. Suddenly there was bright light everywhere; everything glowed. I felt like I had never felt before, wonderful feelings all through my being! Not only did I now have hope, I knew I was in the presence of a heavenly being! I was just outside of this beautiful place, just outside a gate. The gate looked like it was made of pearls and it radiated in beauty, but the light that came from it and from the city inside the gate was unbelievable! It was a light that is not only seen but that penetrates every aspect of your being. The feeling that came over me was so euphoric that nothing in life was sad anymore. I could only feel joy and happiness, no sorrow of any kind.

At this time there was nothing holding on to me like in hell, and I had freedom to move around, so I started to go into the gate. As I moved closer, an angel appeared to me and told me I could not stay in heaven. … I could see everything inside the gates, and I could feel everything everyone else felt, but I wasn't allowed to stay or run around and do things I would have liked. The angel that stopped me at the gate was a massive being, much like a human but larger than life. He had hair down to his shoulders and was wearing some type of white gown that seemed to glow. His hair was sort of very light brown to a dark blonde and by earthly standards of measurement I would say he was about seven feet tall. When he spoke to me, he had the gentlest voice, yet every word had such power with it. It was clear to me at that point how powerful words are, and I instantly thought about the power of God's words when He speaks. It became easy for me to understand how the whole universe was made just by His spoken word.

When we die there is an odd thing that happens. You instantly know things—everything you ever needed to know, you now know. It would be kind of like being given an entire encyclopedia and knowing everything in it in less than a second. No one has to tell you anything or describe anything to you; you just know it through your whole being. Our spirit, as I have learned, doesn't have a brain to mess things up. We get the same thinking capacity as heavenly beings have without our brains trying to analyze everything first; you just know it and accept it. This beautiful angel began to tell me some things about my life and what I need to do when I get back on earth. When he spoke to me, I understood everything and knew exactly what I was supposed to do **when I was sent back,**

yet I wanted to stay. Many things he told to me or showed me I cannot discuss with you yet as I was told to keep them to myself until a time when I will be told it's okay to share it. However, there are some things I can share with you at this time.

I was given several gifts in heaven. One gift is to be able to see inside a person, deep into their soul or spirit. This is not something that I turn on or off, nor can I select the person I can see into; that is up to God. This is not just reserved for church—it happens all the time at work, play, shopping, or anywhere I go. I know it sounds kind of freaky, but it was given to me for a reason. When God gives you a gift, whether it may be singing, teaching, preaching, a kind spirit, a pleasant voice—no matter what it is, use it! God gives us all different gifts, and I know it hurts Him when He sees people who won't use what He gave them or use it for the wrong purpose, but His gifts are irrevocable. What I see is the person's spirit, especially during times of worship. There are many things I see that I never say to a person unless the Holy Spirit gives me the go-ahead; that's just how it works.

I was also shown things about the future. I saw what seemed like millions of people connected to each other with these things at desks and on their laps, and they were typing on them. Remember now, this was in back the '70s and personal com-

puters and laptops did not exist back then. I saw people all over the world connected by something like a big net linking them to each other. People could connect with other people and talk to them through these devices and see the other person on their little TVs. In 1978, many of these things seemed very strange to me. People were walking around talking to each other on phones that had no wires attached, and later with these little things stuck in the ear, and then later in time people were talking into thin air; nothing I could see was attached to them. Then it was shown to me that they had this little device that had been implanted inside their ear with a little machine and all they had to do was tap on the back or bottom of their ear and say a person's name and they could talk to that person.

There was another device that looked like a small, flat TV that was very thin that people walked around with, talking to it and typing on it. There were many people who were all alone, walking and looking at these little phones or flat TVs, typing on them, talking into them. So many people had forgotten how to really communicate, and this was all part of the devil's plan to get control of people because if they forgot how to communicate verbally then they would forget how to pray as well. Connect and keep them in touch with machines instead of people. I also saw buildings in space circling the earth as well as other things I will discuss as I am given permission to do so.[25]

ANGELS, MUSIC, AND MORE

In heaven I learned that are many different types of angels. One type of angel is much like you and me; they are about the same size as our spirits and they look like us. These angels are given unique assignments to specific people and they can be assigned more than one person at a time. I call them Helper angels. They are there to help you through different things in your life on earth. They can transform into looking just like you, if need be. There are also Guardian angels. They are usually assigned to one person at a time and they are there to physically guard you from harm. You have heard people tell stories about how they were heading into an accident that couldn't be avoided and the next thing they knew they were outside of the accident unharmed. That is because of these Guardian angels. Sometimes, though, these angels cannot perform their assignment because the person they are watching over has done something to where the angel can't do their job

---

[25] Ibid., 32-34.

anymore. I will try to explain more on this later.

There are also angels with feathers, or Winged angels. They are usually sent with a particular message to bring to a person or group of people. For example, Winged angels were the ones who announced Jesus' birth, and they are the ones mentioned many times in the Bible who give someone a message from God. I'm sure most of you have heard about angels that show up at places in different churches around the world; that is usually this type of angel. There are also other very important angels that don't have wings that can also bring messages to people; it's just that most messengers are Winged angels.

There are angels whose only assignment is to take answers to prayers back to you. When you pray for something, these angels will be the ones to give you the answers directly from heaven. Some of these angels have been seen, but mostly they are unseen as they carry the message or answer to your prayer. They are very common, and are ascending and descending all the time, 24 hours around the clock. These angels can't make you accept the answers they bring back; that is determined by your will and choice. Archangels are the biggest and most powerful angels. They usually have one assignment at a time and that assignment usually changes life as we know it here on earth. When you come into the presence of an Archangel you can feel its power; you know they represent God firsthand. The power they possess can actually change the course of time and events here on earth. If you saw an Archangel here on earth it would scare you to death.

But in heaven, your spirit understands this power and that its power comes from God, not to be feared in heaven. There were very few Archangels that I saw; only three of them were visible to me. I also saw angels whose only purpose is to worship God. They just sing praises to God and their voices are, well, angelic. There is no other way to explain it; their voices combined together would make anyone hearing it feel euphoric. I saw many more angels there. I didn't know their specific purposes. I only understood the few I just described. There are just so many things that can be understood in the spirit that can never be put into words through the processes of one's mind because the human brain simply can't comprehend it.

The music in heaven is not like what we heard in churches back while I was growing up, or even the new contemporary music back in the '70s; it was more like chants and praises! I can tell you that songs like "Holy" that Jesus Culture sings and some music from Elevation and other groups now is more like what you hear in heaven, but without the heavy electric guitar.

It is total worship. The kind of music is all praise music, not like "The Old Rugged Cross" or hymns; everything is happy and praise-style sounds. Think about it—you are in heaven, God and Jesus are there, and you have everything you could ever want or need, so why not praise!

Here on earth we get tired of things in a short time, but in heaven the people there are so full of the Spirit of God—because they are completely spirit and have no fleshly mind to tire them out or bring them down—that it's 24/7 praise and worship! I tried a lot of different drugs back in the '70s, and there wasn't anything that could give you even one one-millionth of a percent of a high like you get in heaven. Without your flesh to hold you back or to bring thoughts of sinful things into your mind, there is nothing but praise and worship left in you. Your spirit wells up and you just start singing and praising God![26]

DEEPER EXPERIENCES IN HEAVEN

There were some other things I was shown in heaven about the future of our earth. There were people on earth who were there strictly to corrupt the world, the leaders, and the com-

---

[26] Ibid., 37-38.

mon people. These people were possessed of a spirit that leads people into false hopes and delusions. Many people on earth believed these leaders as they convinced the people of earth that everything would be good for them if they just trusted them.

Homosexuality was coming to a peak in the future where it seemed the majority of people were accepting it and the ones who didn't were actually being persecuted and prosecuted in many parts of the world. This angered God! The other spirit that was entering into people caused them to lust after children, and parents gave their children away to others who said they loved their children. Some parents even sold their children to these evil and vile people. Not only were men seeking these children, but women, too. Some wanted to perform homosexual acts on these children and others heterosexual sexual acts on them. This was being accepted in many parts of the world, and it greatly angered God, too!

There was another spirit of lust that was prevalent in the world and that was a lust for power and control. This lust came out of the Middle East and was spreading around the world at an alarming rate. It was disguised as a form of religion and relied heavily on recruiting young people believing in the lies they were told of wonderful places and experiences they would have if they just obeyed. It was the ultimate mind control of our youth.

An army was being raised to take over the world one place at a time, but wearing down all the earth as much as possible. Many of these were little children. From the time of their birth, they were told that Christians were the enemy. Some of these children attended schools that taught them not to love anyone who was not of their faith, but to hate them. However, this spirit of lust for control and power will never be successful because the Spirit of God will not allow it, and the people of this earth will eventually revolt.

I saw Israel standing alone; many nations had separated themselves from Israel, yet Israel had done nothing wrong to deserve it. Even the United States was taking action that harmed Israel. I saw many European nations take a stand against Israel as well. All these European nations and the United States finally turned things around, but only after some damage was already done. These nations changed their minds after they realized they had been lied to and used. **I saw lies, lies, and more lies coming out of the Middle East.** Many of the things I saw then, in my visit to heaven, have now come to pass and have angered God. The people of the earth need a wakeup call, and that is coming soon. The angel showed me that there are a few people on earth right now that know about these things and that they are the intercessors praying for our country. These are not necessarily the big evangelists or TV preachers, but regular individuals who are the intercessors on their face before the Lord daily.

Another thing that was shown to me was the spirit of deception within the church, accompanied by the spirit of self-righteousness. There were people of all religions belonging to churches who were going around trying to divide up the church in order to satisfy their own righteousness. They would go to other individuals in the church and spread lies and rumors about certain ministers in the church, attacking the pastors and worship leaders. These rumors would spread like wildfire. Even those who knew better would start believing because the spirit of deception was so strong, and the people of the church were not prayed up enough to know the difference. Satan is well aware that if he can divide the church, he can conquer it and steal people away. However, this too will come to a stop by the power of the Holy Spirit. The people trying to do this will be exposed and they will be accountable for the ones they led astray unless they repent.

Something else the angel talked to me about was **hidden intentional sin. These are sins that people who claim to be**

Christians do frequently on a regular basis. Let me explain—if you are a Christian, you know right from wrong from the Holy Spirit indwelling within you.

But if you think that right and wrong are only what other people see in you, you are deceiving yourself. What has been happening is that many people are claiming one thing and behind closed doors are doing another. If you are looking at porn, treating your family badly, cheating on your spouse, are into violent or graphic gaming, using illegal drugs or abusing prescription drugs, or drinking alcoholic beverages daily, and you are hiding these things, then that is your hidden intentional sin. These are not the only ones; there are many more, like aggravating your children, lusting after your fellow coworker, cussing, anything that you would not do in front of Jesus if He were standing next to you. Doing these things over and over again when you know it is wrong—that is intentional sinning. Hidden intentional sinning has become one of the worst epidemics in the Christian community; it surpasses anything close to it by a mile.

The angel said that this displeases God greatly and He wants it made known. He said that if people do not repent, then He will expose them, from the top evangelist on down to the quietest person at church. I want to further elaborate that I am not talking about sin that is unintentional; I am talking about sin that you know is wrong, yet you intentionally choose to repeat the behavior. You are not fooling anyone but yourself. Believe it or not, many times people know that you are doing it, but they don't say anything because they don't want to embarrass you. Don't you think you are going to hate it when it is exposed to everyone and they all find out what you are doing? I mean, what if you are beating your spouse, looking at porn or lusting after someone while you are married—do you really want that exposed? Do you?

I have been charged with warning you because I have been there, and you don't want to go to hell! I am being sent with this warning—either you repent and change your ways, or it will be exposed. The time for you to take heed to what I am saying is now; you have been warned by reading this book. Let me ask you a question—if you saw a three-year-old child walking along the side of the road and they turn to walk directly into oncoming traffic going 75 miles per hour, what would you do? Would you just keep driving away looking in the other direction and hope someone else will stop and help them, or think maybe they will magically make it through to the other side? I would be willing to bet most of you would come to a screeching halt, jump out of your car, and rescue them. That is what I am doing by warning you about this. This is the most stoppable sin there is, because you already know it's wrong and you know the right way to go, so please stop before it's too late! You have no idea how many people I saw in hell who didn't belong there —or at least, they didn't think they did. Hidden intentional sin has been rampant for many years now and getting worse every day, especially with all the new technology continually coming out. In the near future this technology will even produce human-like forms that will be part of the worst lust the word has ever seen.[27]

BACK TO EARTH

I do want to tell you more about **why I was spared from hell**, and it has nothing to do with me or my cries for help while in hell. **The angel that spoke to me in heaven also told me that God was honoring my mother's prayers because she had been so faithful to God in her life and had said over 20,000 prayers for me, and God made her a promise about her children. She prayed for me two to three times daily. Can you imagine being prayed for 20,000 times?** My mother is a godly woman and

---

[27] Ibid., 43-47.

brought all of her children up in the ways of the Lord and in church. The paths we took may not have been right, but she knew that if she raised us in the ways of the Lord we would all return someday if we drifted away. Mom, you were right about that one!

This angel explained to me that everyone who goes to hell cries out for God but that it is too late for them. My escape from hell was one in a million, and it wasn't because of anything I did on earth or how I lived. It's because it wasn't my time to die, and because of my mother's prayers. Parents, never stop praying for your children. Even when it looks impossible, keep praying for them and never give up.[28]

FINAL WORDS

There are many more things that were revealed to me, and sometime soon I will be writing more about them, but in the meantime **take heed what the Spirit of God has revealed. Those of you with hidden intentional sin need to get on your face before the Lord and repent, which means to not only ask for forgiveness but to change your ways. The warning about hidden**

---

[28] Ibid., 48.

intentional sin is a very stern warning and it has been given in order to save your life, not to embarrass you nor condemn you. God does not want your sin to be revealed to everyone. He just wants you to repent, in private if necessary, and change your lifestyle. God loves you![29]

---

[29] Ibid., 75.

9

George Lennox

Although I have heard many stories about people dying and coming back to life, the one that interested me the most was the true story of George Lennox.

DEATH OF A CRIMINAL

George Lennox worked in a prison coal mine during the winter of 1887–1888. The room that he had worked in seemed dangerous to him. He reported this to the officer in charge, who examined the room. Deciding that the room was safe, the officer ordered Lennox back to work.

Lennox had not worked for more than an hour when the roof fell in and completely buried him. He remained in that condition for around two hours. As he was missed at dinnertime, a search was made for him. He was found under a pile of rubbish, and it looked like he was dead. He was taken to another area and examined by the prison physician, who pronounced him dead. His body was carried to the hospital where it was washed and dressed for interment. His coffin was made and brought to the hospital.

UNEXPECTED RESURRECTION

The chaplain had arrived to perform the last sad rites preparatory to burial. The hospital steward ordered two prisoners to lift the corpse and carry it across the room and place it in the coffin. They obeyed. One was at the head and the other at the feet, and they were about halfway across the room when the one who was at the head accidentally stumbled over a cuspidor, lost his balance, and dropped the corpse. The head of the dead man struck the floor, and to the utter surprise and astonishment of all those who were there, a deep groan was heard.

The physician was immediately sent for. When he arrived around thirty minutes later, Lennox was drinking a cup of water. The coffin was removed, and it was used later to bury another inmate. Lennox's burial clothes were taken from him and prison garb was given to him instead. Upon examination, it was discovered that one of his legs was broken in two places, and he also had some bruises. He remained in the hospital for six months before he went back to work.

THE TESTIMONY OF GEORGE LENNOX

"I had a premonition all morning that something terrible was going to happen. I was so uneasy on account of my feelings that I went to my mining boss, Mr. Grason, and told him how I felt. I asked him to examine my room where I was digging coal. He did so, and seemed to make a thorough examination of it. He then ordered me back to work, saying there was no danger and that he thought I was going nuts. I returned to my work and dug coal for about an hour, when suddenly it grew very dark. Then it seemed as if a great iron door swung open and I passed through it.

The thought came to my mind that I was dead and in another world. I could see no one, nor hear sound of any kind. From some cause unknown to myself, I moved away from the doorway and traveled some distance when I came to the bank of a wide river. It was not dark, neither was it light. There was about as much light as on a bright, starlit night.

I had not remained on the bank of this river very long when

I heard the sound of oars in the water, and then a person in a boat rowed up to where I was standing. I was speechless. He looked at me for a moment and then said that he had come for me, and told me to get into the boat and row to the other side of the river. I obeyed. I wanted to ask him who he was and where I was, but my tongue seemed to cling to the roof of my mouth. I could not say a word.

The Narrow Path and the Wide Path

We finally reached the opposite shore. I got out of the boat and the boatman vanished out of sight. As I was left alone, I knew not what to do. I saw **two roads** in front of me **that led through a dark valley. One of these roads was wide, and it seemed to be well traveled. The other one was a narrow path, which went in another direction.** I instinctively followed the well-traveled road. I had not gone far when it seemed to grow darker.

Every now and then, however, a light would flash up from the distance, and in this manner I was lighted on my journey.

Guided by a Demon

I was then met by a being that is utterly impossible for me to describe. I can only give you a faint idea of his dreadful appear-

ance. He somewhat resembled a man but was much larger than any human being I ever saw. He must have been at least ten feet high. He had great wings on his back. He was as black as the coal that I had been digging and in a perfectly nude condition. He had a spear in his hand, the handle of which must have been fully fifteen feet in length. His eyes shone like balls of fire. His teeth, white as pearl, seemed an inch long. His nose, if you could call it a nose, was very large, broad and flat. His hair was very coarse, heavy and long. It hung down on his massive shoulders. His voice sounded like the growls of a lion. I trembled like an aspen leaf at his sight. He had his spear raised as if to send it flying through me. With his terrible voice (that I seem to yet hear), he told me to follow him—that he had been sent to guide me on my journey. I followed. What else could I do?

Here Is Hell!

After we had gone some distance, a large mountain seemed to rise up before us. The part facing us seemed perpendicular, just as if the mountain had been cut in two and one part had been taken away. On this perpendicular wall I could distinctly see these words: **This is Hell.** My guide approached this perpendicular wall and gave three loud raps with his spear handle. A massive door swung open and we went in. I was then led through what appeared to be a passage through this mountain.

For some time we traveled in total darkness. I could hear the heavy footsteps of my guide and so I followed him. All along the way I could hear deep groans as if someone was dying. Further on these groans increased, and I could distinctly hear the cry, 'water, water, water.' Coming now to another gateway, and passing through it, I could hear, it seemed, a million voices in the distance, crying for water. Another large door opened at the knock of my guide, and I saw that we had passed through the mountain, and a wide plain was now before me. My guide then left me to direct other lost spirits to the same destination.

I remained in this open plain for a while when a being somewhat similar to the first one came to me, but instead of a spear he had a huge sword.

This Will Soon Be Your Doom

He came to tell me of my future doom. He spoke with a voice that struck horror to my soul. He said, **'You are in hell—for you, all hope has fled away. As you passed through the mountain on your way here, you heard the groans and shrieks of lost spirits as they called for water to cool their parched tongues.**

Along that passage there is a door that opens to the lake of fire.

This will soon be your doom. Before you are conducted to this place of torment, never more to emerge, (for there is no hope for those who enter there), you will be permitted to remain in this open plain, where it is granted to all the lost to behold what they might have enjoyed instead of what they must suffer." I was then left alone.

Whether the result of the terrible fright through which I had passed I know not, but now I became stupefied. A dull languor took full possession of me. My strength departed from me. My legs refused to support my body. Being overcome with this, I sank down into a helpless mess. Drowsiness now took control of me. Half awake, half asleep, I seemed to dream.

The Beautiful City Made of Jasper

Far above me, and in the distance, I saw the Beautiful City of which we read about in the Bible. How wonderfully beautiful were its walls of jasper. I saw vast plains covered with beautiful flowers stretching way out in the distance. I also saw the River of Life and the Sea of Glass. Vast multitudes of angels would go in and out through the gates of that city, singing, oh, such beautiful songs. I saw my dear old mother, who died a few years ago of a broken heart because of my wickedness. She looked toward me and seemed to beckon me to come to her, but I could not move. There seemed to be a great weight on me that held me down. A gentle breeze blew the fragrance of those lovely flowers toward me, and I could now clearly hear the sweet melody of angel's voices, and I said to myself, 'Oh, if I could only be one of them.'

The Lake of Fire and Brimstone

As I was drinking from this cup of bliss, it was suddenly dashed from my lips. I was aroused from my slumber in happy dreamland by an inmate of that dark abode, who said that it was time for me to enter upon my future career. He told me to follow him. Retracing my steps, I again entered the dark passageway and followed my guide. We came to a door that opened in the side of the passage, and going further along we found and passed through another door, and lo, I beheld the Lake of Fire!

Just before me, as far as my eyes could see, was that literal lake of fire and brimstone. Huge waves of fire would roll over each other, and great waves of fiery flame would dash against each other and leap high in the air like the waves of the sea during a violent storm. On the crest of those waves I could see human beings rising up, but were soon carried down again to the lowest depths of that awful lake of fire.

Their curses against a just God would be appalling, and their pitiful cries for water would be heart-rending, as they were carried along on the crest of those awful waves. That vast region of fire echoed and re-echoed with the wails of those lost spirits.

I turned my eyes to the door through which I had a few moments ago entered, and I saw these awful words: This is your doom. Eternity never ends! I began to feel the earth give way under my feet, and I found myself sinking down into the Lake of Fire. An indescribable thirst for water seized me, and as I called for water my eyes opened in the prison hospital.

Now I'm a New Creation!

I have never told anyone my experience, for I feared the prison officials would get hold of it, think me insane, and lock me up in the madhouse. **I went through all of it, and I am as well satisfied as I am that I am alive, that there is a Heaven and a Hell—a regular old-fashioned Hell—the kind the Bible talks about. But there is one thing for sure—I am never going back to that place.**

As soon as I opened my eyes in the hospital and found out that I was alive and on earth again, I immediately gave my heart to God, and I am going to live and die a Christian. Those terrible sights of Hell can never be banished from my memory, neither can the beautiful things of Heaven that I saw.

I am going to meet my dear old mother after awhile. To be permitted to sit down on the bank of that beautiful river, to wander with those angels across the plains and through the vales and over the hills carpeted with fragrant flowers, the beauty of which far surpasses anything that any mortal can imagine; to listen to the songs of the saved—all this will more than compensate me for living the life of a Christian here on earth, even if I have to give up many sensual pleasures in which I indulged before coming to prison. I have abandoned my companions in crime and I am going to associate with good people when I am once more a free man."[30]

---

[30] John Reynolds, "48 Hours in Hell" (2022, December 15). Free Holiness Gospel Literature. https://freeholinessgospelliterature.com/christian-tracts/48-hours-in-hell/

The Final Appeal!

Beloved, how were the testimonies? As far as I'm concerned, I believe many of you have repented, chosen to believe in Jesus, and have formed a desire to go to heaven and not hell after reading these testimonies.

Yet, sadly, some might be thinking the following.

'Of course I need to believe in Jesus if this is the truth! But how can I be sure that stories like this about heaven and hell are not delusions and actually true?'

However, you can be sure. The evidence is when Jean Darnall's mother amazingly recognized her own mother. Moreover, we see it through Elder Young-moon Park's experience, which happened to him when he was still a non-believer and hated Christians. It was also a dramatic experience that happened right before he almost completely wiped out his wife's family. There would be no reason to make it up.

Nevertheless, I want to introduce to you one last testimony for those who are still in doubt. It is from the most recent book that I read, *My Time in Heaven,* which talks about the after-life experience of Richard Sigmund. For a long time, I had not read testimonies on heaven and hell. But while compiling this book, I became interested in them again and looked them up. That is when I found the following author's bio of Richard Sigmund, and it deeply moved me.

"**Richard Sigmund (1941–2010) was born in Des Moines, Iowa. … As a child, he started preaching… and Rev. Coe brought Richard to Omaha in 1949 to preach. When he was about nine years old, he presented the gospel before the meetings of world-renowned evangelist and miracle worker A. A. Allen. Richard was with Allen for about ten years. … Also during that time, Richard was with evangelist Lee Girard and presented his testimony during William Branham meetings. In his early twenties, Richard had a fruitful ministry for a time in Phoenix, Arizona, and then held tent meetings with considerable success among the Navajo in northern Arizona and in other revival meetings around the country.**

In 1974, while he was ministering at a small church in Bar-

tlesville, Oklahoma, he was declared dead for eight hours after a traffic accident, during which he had his experiences of heaven and hell. Over the years, Richard preached the gospel through television programs, radio broadcasts, and speaking engagements. He was in meetings with Kathryn Kuhlman and Oral Roberts… Richard ministered in England, Scotland, Australia, South Africa, Kenya, and many other countries."[31]

Is it not truly spectacular? So, after reading this introduction, I immediately bought his book and read it.

Richard Sigmund died in a traffic accident on October 17th, 1974. During that time, he saw heaven and hell and then came back to life. And through his experience, we see much evidence that backs up how real it all was.

First, ever since he was young, Sigmund experienced a special grace of God.

"Jesus told me, **'When you were a child, I came to you.'**
When I was seven years old, I saw Jesus come down on a golden stairway. When I was four years old, I was caught

---

31 Richard Sigmund, *My Time in Heaven*, (New Kensington, PA: Whitaker House, 1999) 142-143. Kindle Edition.

away to heaven while I was at my grandfather's house. My grandfather was quite a gentleman and a Bible reader. He was a protégé of evangelist Billy Sunday; they were great friends. That day, I had gone outside to catch grasshoppers... I remember reaching down to pick up a grasshopper, and the next thing I knew, I was in heaven standing before the throne of God.

I'll never forget it—there were royal purple tapestries everywhere and big columns.

Jesus was sitting on the throne, and He looked down at me and smiled. He said, 'Never drink, never smoke, never sin—there's work for you to do later on.'

Then, I remember jumping... Now, in my heavenly audience with the Master, Jesus said to me, 'I have called you as a prophet to the nations. In many ways, you have succeeded. In many ways, the evil one hindered and overcame you. But fear not; I have overcome him. **I was there when you were born. I was there when you were four and the evil one tried to destroy you.'**

As a young child, I had contracted measles, scarlet fever, and other sicknesses. The doctor had given up on me. My mother was rocking me while my dad was in the field plowing. Suddenly, the house filled with smoke as if it was on fire, but there was no smell of fire. My mother cried out, 'God, if You spare this boy...' Out of the cloud came two hands that healed me."[32]

Second, his revival from death to life was in itself a miracle.

"There was a sheet over my face. Oh, did I hurt!

'He's been dead all these hours,' I heard. I sat up and said, 'I ain't dead yet.' A medical attendant screamed. Another lost bladder control. Apparently, I had been dead for over eight hours, and they were wheeling me down to the morgue. **I could feel my bones knitting together. I could feel the scars healing while I sat up**. And I breathed and spoke."[33]

Sigmund further explained this later in his book.

"Jesus said, 'You are going back.' ...

Then, Jesus hugged me. **Suddenly, my body was full of pain. There was a sheet over my face. I could feel my bones knitting together; I was being healed**. I heard a voice say, 'He's been

---

[32] Sigmund, *My Time in Heaven*, 88-89.
[33] Ibid., 14.

dead all these hours.'

I could feel my left wrist where the bone had been protruding—I could feel it popping into place and healing up. 'It is about time to embalm him.' I remember sitting up and saying, 'I ain't dead yet.'

Someone hollered in the hall, 'He's alive! That dead man is alive!' I remember a doctor coming in and saying, 'I pronounced him dead, and he is dead.'

But I was sitting up. Other doctors and nurses came in, and I began to tell the story of where I had been and what had happened. People were weeping. Doctors said, **'This must be a miracle of God.'"** [34]

Third, there is evidence that what he saw in heaven was not a hallucination, but reality. When Richard Sigmund died and went to heaven, God showed him the following.

"I was taken to an avenue named The Way of the Rose. ...**There were some homes still under construction. One of them had names carved in beautiful letters above the entrance. These names were Paul and Judy of the family Heg-**

---

34 Ibid., 100.

strom. **At that time, I didn't know who they were,** and I didn't have the nerve to ask. I noticed that the other homes were of similar construction.

… The main libraries in these houses were lined with books that were embossed with gold. **They were heaven's pre-copies of books that have been written and that will be written in the time to come.**

Of the library at the Hegstrom home, Jesus said to me, 'These books were written by My Spirit at the beginning of time. **They were given to Paul Hegstrom to write on earth when he was there. You will meet him later. When you do, tell him that there is much to do and not to slacken the pace.'** …

On the front of the Hegstrom home was a memorial to the glory that God had received from the yielded life of this man. **Again, I was made to know that I would meet him later, in his season."**[35]

So, do you think he was able to meet them after coming back to life? Surprisingly, he was able to meet them. He said the following about it in his book.

---

35 Ibid., 47-48.

"Fulfillment of Heavenly Prophecy

Over the years, every once in a while, I have met someone whom I was told in heaven that I would meet on earth. One of those people is Paul Hegstrom, whose heavenly home I'd seen under construction on the avenue named 'The Way of the Rose,' and whose heavenly library contained the books he would write. (See chapter 8.)

I met Paul through pioneer television evangelist Dr. L. D. Kramer, who is a friend of mine. L. D. mentioned Paul's name to me, and I said, 'I know that name.' Then, I told him what had happened to me and how I had seen the names of Paul and his wife, Judy, on their home under construction in heaven. Since L. D. Kramer was well-known, he got in touch with Paul on my behalf, and he came down to see me in Texas. …

I told him the names of the books I'd seen in his heavenly library, and he said, 'We're just now writing those books!'" [36]

Fourth, Sigmund did not only see heaven and hell, but great miracles followed in his ministry.

---

[36] Ibid., 102-103.

"**Supernatural Manifestations and Increased Ministry**

Since my heavenly experience, I have continued to have visitations of the Lord. God has poured out His Spirit into my life. **I have witnessed the blind see, the deaf hear, and the lame walk, and I have literally seen the dead raised.** A man dropped dead across from my driveway. By the time the ambulance arrived, **the man hadn't breathed for fifteen minutes, but, after prayer, he came back to life.**

In another case, a man was working on building a church in Mexico when an adobe brick fell on his head and crushed his skull. **He died instantly. Everyone gathered around him and prayed, and God raised him up. Then, he said, 'I was in heaven, and I didn't want to come back!'** ...

There have been other miracles, as well. There was a man in the hospital who had a broken leg, which the doctors couldn't seem to realign so that it could heal. They called my friend Pastor Randy Wallace and me to come and pray. **God set that bone before our very eyes, and his leg was healed.**

In every service, I see the outpouring of the Holy Spirit and God performing the miraculous. When I tell my story, there are always a great number of people who want to get right with God."[37]

---

[37] Ibid., 101-2.

Is this not amazing? However, this is just a portion of the wonderful miracles that happened through him. Beloved, do you still believe that his testimony is just a delusion? His testimony is real. In other words, heaven and hell truly exist. Sigmund said the following about hell.

"I quickly realized that hell is the exact opposite of everything that heaven is. The gates were as big as the gates in heaven, but these were made of a black material. ... And there were hideous, grotesque beings as tall as the angels who guarded the gates of heaven. Some cartoon figures of demons approach how hideous these creatures were. ...

There were also flames of punishment. I felt the doom and despair there. I heard people crying out. It seems that demons take people and torture them to the same level of pain the demons themselves are in—or worse....

Jesus urged me to tell people what I saw. **'I want you to tell others of this place and warn them that unless they are washed in My blood, unless they are born again, this is where they will spend eternity.'**

There were demons all around... There were people begging and pleading with Jesus to get them out of there, but He would not hear them because their judgment was fixed. (See Hebrews 9:27.) **I cannot describe everything I saw because it makes me violently ill. I don't want to remember.** But I can tell you that there is absolute horror.

When you die, you have a spiritual body. This spiritual body has the exact properties that your physical body had when you were alive. You are a spirit being, yet all physical senses are present.

I saw people in hell who were no more than walking skeletons with flesh of some kind hanging off of them—rotting off of them. There were maggots, and the smell was unbreathable. People were being raped. Serpents ate and digested parts of people; then, the people were restored and it happened all over again.

I witnessed people being ripped apart by demons. Parts of their bodies were hanging on boulders and rocks, and the demons would take the parts and eat them and pass them through. And then the body was whole again for the process to be repeated.

A young girl had hot coals forced into her mouth as demons mocked, 'You really thought you were getting by with something.'

There were groups of people in small cages that were on

fire. People were put into small, burning cages that were then dipped in a lake of fire. However, their bodies were not consumed. The bodies were never consumed. They were half skeletons/half beings.

Demons poured liquid fire on people. There were what looked like coal pits burning. People had cancer, with all its pain and suffering—forever.

One man had a rotting arm. It took a hundred years to rot off. Then, it was restored, only to begin rotting off again.

There was another man with part of his head blown off from war. He had to keep looking for the rest of his head. ... Every torment you can imagine is multiplied a million times. There are degrees of punishment in hell."[38]

Is this not horrific and terrifying? Yet, this is the very place we will spend eternity in if we do not repent of our sins and believe in Jesus. It is why I have published this book, for I cannot sit here and watch this happen to you.

To those who love God: it is a great blessing you are alive and I am so glad you are. For when you die, there will never be another chance. Moreover, we do not know what lies ahead in our lives,

---

[38] Ibid., 90-92.

not even what will happen the next day. This might be the last chance you have to avoid hell and go to heaven. Therefore, please, I beg you to not lose this chance. Make the decision to believe in Jesus like Young-moon Park and George Lennox did! And I hope that you will sincerely pray the following prayer with me.

"Jesus, who is the son of the living God and our Savior!
I am a sinner and a being in need of salvation.
I do not want to go to hell.
I want to go to heaven.
So, I will rely on the cross,
And receive you Jesus as my Lord and Saviour.
Wash away my sins with your blood,
And allow me to be born again through the Spirit and become a child of God.
Be with me from now until I go to heaven, and guide me.
I thank you for forgiving my sins and for saving me.
From now on, I will live for you Lord, and will live according to God's will.
I pray all this in Jesus' name. Amen."

Beloved, you have done well! Now, go out to the closest church in your neighborhood this coming Sunday. And take part in the

Christian life till the very end. I pray that by doing so, you will certainly not go to hell, and that instead, we will all meet each other in heaven!